T0271591

CAUGHT SNACKIN'

CAUGHT SNACKIN'

hamlyn

**100 RECIPES.
SIMPLE. FAST. FLAVOURSOME.**

First published in Great Britain in 2023 by Hamlyn, an imprint of
Octopus Publishing Group Ltd
Carmelite House
50 Victoria Embankment
London EC4Y 0DZ
www.octopusbooks.co.uk

An Hachette UK Company
www.hachette.co.uk

ISBN 9-780-60063-756-1

A CIP catalogue record for this book is available from the British Library.

Printed and bound in China.

10 9 8 7 6 5 4 3 2 1

Publicity Director: Eleanor Maxfield
Art Director: Yasia Williams
Designer: Abigail Read
Senior Editor: Pollyanna Poulter
Copy Editor: Lucy Bannell
Production Managers: Lucy Carter and Nic Jones
Photographer: Louise Hagger
Prop Stylist: Alexander Breeze
Food Stylist: Becks Wilkinson

CONTENTS

INTRODUCTION

Caught Snackin' was launched on TikTok in April 2020 by the gang with a love for food! Two years later, we're the UK's fastest-growing TikTok channel, finessin' the game with recipe films that SLAP! You know like that?

OBVIOUSLY we had to roll through with Snackin' the cookbook. Snackin's where we started, but our cookbook covers all bases: from bougie brunches to simple lunches, Friday-night fakeaways to desserts that will make you TikTok famous.

Whether you're new to the kitchen or looking to level up, Caught will bless you! You don't need mad chefileeni equipment or Gordon Ramsay tekz, just this book and good vibes.

This book is made for everyone: we believe that home-cooked food is the best way to eat, and anyone can do it with the right recipe. Our dishes are created firstly for deliciousness and secondly for easel; whether you're going all-in cooking for a crowd or cotching on the sofa with a bowl full of comfort food, we're bringing big flavours with zero stress. Our inspo came from all kinds of places and faces: TikTok, friends of Caught, food our families cooked, and random kitchen experiments gone RIGHT. It took us 730 DAYS and 1,500 dishes to get to where we are (with a few burnt fingers and dud dishes along the way, not gonna lie). We're buzzing for you lot to get cooking and eat this sensational food with us, you get me?

Just a few things for the gang to know...

The book is split into seven tasty chapters: Snackin' for the quick munch, Brunchin' for them strong starts to the day, Lunchin' for an upgrade from your meal deal, Dinin' for the winner dinners, Fakin' for the HACKS, Bakin' for them sweeeet treats and Sippin' for drinks too good not to share.

Our servings range from one to four people, but every appetite is different, so you do you. We don't judge! If you finesse a four-person recipe between two of you, it's calm. If you want to upsize or downsize, just adjust the servings to suit, or if you have an urge to freestyle and add your own spin on something, then we love to see it.

Importantly, our ingredients don't cost too much. Whether you're living the student life or making bank, our shopping lists suit everyman. Our food is inclusive and will put a smile on the face of everyone, from your nan to the sweet one you want to impress. ESPECIALLY the SWEET ONE.

Right, we're talkin' too much. Time to roll up your sleeves and gear up for some serious snackin'. We hope you love this cookbook as much as we've loved making it; if you do, share the love with your friends and fam. Everyone's welcome in the Caught gang.

Whatever you're feeling, we got you! We hope the pages of this cookbook will soon be folded and flour-dusted from recipes you've gone back to again and again.

LET'S GOOOOO!

CAUGHT STREET GLOSSARY

YES PEOPLE, first things first. Anyone in the Snackin' gang will know how to speak our language, and if you're reading this book, you need to be educated with the lingo. This is worth at least three GCSEs:

BANAYNAY
it's a banana, don't ask questions.

BANGING
amazing.

BASIC-B
generic.

BEV/BEVI
alcoholic/non-alcoholic drink.

BLESS or BLESSED
when something good happens.

BOUJEE
someone who be living that high life. Champagne, oysters and that.

CHEFILEENI
the correct way to say chef.

CHEEEEEEEEEEEEESE
it just means cheese.

CHEF IT UP
cutting/slicing/cooking in general.

COTCHING
chilling.

G
mate, bro, hun, your nearest and dearest.

GLOW-UP
makeover.

MANDEM
the whole gang.

MAZZA
a madness.

MEADY

low-level/substandard.

PATTERNED

sort out/fix up.

PREE

look at.

RAGRETS

regrets, doh.

SAFE

cool/thanks.

SHOOK

this is like scared or shocked.

SHUBZ

party, gathering... anything
with all the Caught gang!

SITCH

situation.

SLAPS

impressive, VERY good, delicious...

SWEET ONE

your lurver.

TEKZ

techniques.

TURNT

excited.

YES PEOPLE

a classic Caught Snackin' greeting
(if you know you know).

Now that's done, WELCOME to the gang!

GET YOUR SHOP ON

**Listen, every chefileeni needs them ingredient staples!
Let us pattern you real quick...**

OILS

- olive oil
- sunflower or vegetable oil

SEASONINGS

- American mustard
- black pepper
- Italian mixed dried herbs
- salt
- soy sauce
- sweet chilli sauce
- tomato ketchup

SPICES

- chilli flakes
- chilli powder
- curry powder
- fresh basil
- fresh coriander
- garam masala
- garlic powder
- ground cinnamon
- ground cumin
- ground turmeric
- onion powder
- smoked paprika

STORE CUPBOARD

- baked beans
- basmati rice
- breadcrumbs (panko)
- canned tomatoes
- chocolate hazelnut spread, such as Nutella
- corn puffs
- dried pasta
- garlic
- instant noodles
- long-grain rice
- onions
- ready-salted crisps
- runny honey
- speculoos biscuits, such as Lotus
- speculoos spread
- sriracha
- stock cubes (veg and chicken)
- tomato purée/paste
- tortilla chips
- tortilla wraps
- white sliced bread
- yeast extract spread, such as Marmite

BAKING

- caster sugar
- condensed milk
- dark chocolate
- icing sugar
- instant cake mix
- jelly cubes
- marshmallows
- milk chocolate
- plain flour
- self-raising flour
- white chocolate

REFRIGERATOR & FREEZER

- butter (salted and unsalted)
- chocolate ice cream
- cream (single or double)
- eggs
- ice cubes
- mayonnaise
- vanilla ice cream
- whole milk
- yogurt

PREP DEM TOOLS

All our recipes use easy equipment that every kitchen should already have (if you don't have an ovenproof dish, then it's a bit of a sticky one still), but here's a list of kit you'll need to get cheffin':

COOKWARE

- baking/cake tin
- baking sheet
- big roasting tin
- couple of decent ovenproof, nonstick frying pans: one shallow, one deep with a proper fitted lid
- deep saucepan with a fitted lid
- large ovenproof dish with a fitted lid
- muffin tray
- ovenproof ramekins

ELECTRICS

- electric whisk
- food processor or high–powered blender
- freezer
- hand–held stick blender
- microwave
- thermometer (handy for deep–frying – if you don't have one, check out our tip on page 17)

KIT

- ice–cube tray
- ovenproof bowls (we recommend 1–litre and 0.5–litre Pyrex heatproof glass bowls)
- piping bag with nozzles
- plastic squeezy sauce bottle with nozzle lid/piping bottle
- rolling pin
- sauce whisk (small hand whisk)
- shot measure

RANDOMS

- tea towels
- kitchen roll
- nonstick baking paper
- foil
- clingfilm
- muffin cases

OK, now you're REALLY ready, so LET'S GO GO GOOOOO!

CAUGHT
SNACKIN'

BASIC COOKING TIPS FOR BEGINNERS

My kitchen rookies, I see you! But don't worry, start with these kitchen tips and you'll soon be flexing mad chefileeni skills!

HOW TO
CHOP AN ONION

1. Using a large, sharp knife, remove the pointed end of the onion. Do not remove the root end, as this holds the onion layers together, making it easier to chop. Slicing the root end off will also release acidic juices, which make you cry.

2. Slice the onion in half horizontally (from end to end) and peel away the tough outer skin.

3. Place an onion half flat–side down and, holding your knife parallel to the work surface, carefully slice through the onion horizontally, taking your knife almost to the root end but not cutting through it completely, so that the onion half remains held together.

4. Now, make a series of cuts through the onion half lengthways, every 5mm (¼ inch) or so, starting from the root end to the pointed end, Again, keeping the root end intact.

5. Finally, holding your knife flat against the pointed end of the onion, slice against the cuts you have just made, resulting in fine dice. Chop along the onion, until you get 1-2cm (½-¾ inch) away from the root. Discard the root.

6. Repeat with the other half.

HOW TO
SWEAT AN ONION

1. Heat 1–2 tablespoons olive oil in a frying pan or saucepan over a low-medium heat and add the finely chopped onion. Season with salt and give it a stir to ensure the onion is coated in oil. Cook for 5 minutes or so, until the onion starts to turn translucent.

2. Tear off a square sheet of nonstick baking paper and scrunch it up into a tight ball. Un–scrunch it and run it under water to dampen, then place it over the onions. It will act as a lid, and the moisture will help the onions sweat and stop them from catching. Reduce the heat to its lowest and allow the onions to sweat for 15-20 minutes, checking them every 5 minutes. The onions are cooked when they are fully translucent with a sweet aroma.

HOW TO MAKE

A SIMPLE TOMATO SAUCE

PREP TIME: **5 MINUTES**   COOK TIME: **40 MINUTES**

DIFFICULTY: **EASY**   SERVES: **2**

VEGAN

INGREDIENTS

1–2 tablespoons olive oil

½ onion, finely chopped

1 carrot, finely chopped

1 celery stick, finely chopped

2 garlic cloves, crushed

1 teaspoon Italian mixed dried herbs

1 tablespoon tomato purée/paste

400 g (14 oz) can of chopped tomatoes

salt and pepper

METHOD

1. Heat the oil in a frying pan or saucepan over a low–medium heat. Add the onion, carrot and celery and season with salt and pepper.

2. Sweat for 15 minutes, until the vegetables have softened, then add the garlic, dried herbs and tomato purée. Stir and cook for 5 minutes.

3. Pour over the chopped tomatoes and bring to a gentle simmer, stirring to combine. Cover and simmer the sauce for 20 minutes.

4. Season to taste and serve with pasta, use as a pizza base sauce, or allow to cool and save for another day. The sauce will keep in the refrigerator for 4 days, or in the freezer for up to 3 months.

You'll soon be flexing mad chefileeni skills!

HOW TO MAKE

A SIMPLE CHEESE SAUCE

PREP TIME: **5 MINUTES**   COOK TIME: **5 MINUTES**

DIFFICULTY: **EASY**   SERVES: **2**

VEGGIE

INGREDIENTS

25 g (1 oz) unsalted butter

25 g (1 oz) plain flour

250–300 ml (9 fl oz–½ pint) milk

small pinch of ground nutmeg (optional)

80 g (2¾ oz) grated Cheddar cheese

salt and pepper

METHOD

1. Melt the butter in a saucepan over a medium heat. Add the flour and whisk it into the butter until you have a thick, smooth paste. A sauce whisk (smaller than a normal whisk) is best for this. Cook the paste, whisking, for about 2 minutes until it turns a pale biscuit colour. This is called a 'roux' (pronounced 'roo') and is a classic base to all white sauces.

2. Slowly pour in the milk, a little at a time, whisking it into the roux before adding the next splash of milk. Once all the milk is incorporated, increase the heat a little and allow it to thicken slightly for 2 minutes before seasoning with salt and pepper.

3. If you wish to make a simple bechamel sauce, stop here, adding a small pinch of ground nutmeg. Great for homemade lasagne. If carrying on to make a cheese sauce, simply add the grated Cheddar and stir through over a low heat until fully melted. For a simple macaroni and cheese, stir through par–boiled pasta shells and bake in the oven, topped with more cheese and breadcrumbs (see our hack on page 88 for how to make your own breadcrumbs).

Cheeeeeeeeeeeeesy

DEEP-FRYING
HOW TO CHECK THE TEMPERATURE OF OIL WITHOUT A THERMOMETER

When deep-frying, we recommend you use a temperature probe/cooking thermometer to check the oil temperature for safety and precision. These are easily purchased online or in cookware shops and some of the larger supermarkets. However, if you don't have one, you can check the temperature using a less precise method... bread!

When the oil is hot (this will take 5–10 minutes over a low–medium heat) drop in a cube of bread. The oil should bubble around the edges of the bread, and the bread will start to take on colour as it cooks. The length of time the bread takes to turn a deep golden colour is a good indicator of the temperature of the oil:

30 seconds = 160°C (325°F)
15 seconds = 180°C (350°F)
10 seconds = 190°C (375°F)

We recommend deep-frying with either vegetable oil or sunflower oil, as these have a high smoke point (so are less likely to burn).

· ·

SAFETY ADVICE

Don't own a deep-fryer? Use a large saucepan with a well-fitting lid. **Only use the lid when you have finished cooking and the saucepan has been removed from the heat.** Putting a lid on a pan of boiling oil can lead to dangerously high temperatures. Plus, it will result in sweaty, soggy food, and lose you that all-important crunch.

Keep a plate lined with kitchen paper nearby so that you can remove fried food and drain it without dripping hot oil all over the kitchen.

Use a metal slotted or wire-mesh spoon to remove food from hot oil.

NEVER mix water with hot oil, as this will cause a fire. Be sure to keep any water or other liquids away from the hot oil.

If the oil becomes too hot, the safest way to cool it down is to add cold oil and remove the pan from the heat.

Hot oil takes a long time to cool down (a few hours), so leave it in a safe place in your kitchen, covered with a well-fitting lid and out of reach of young children.

Always ensure there is an adult present when deep-frying. SAFE.

WILDFIRE HALLOUMI FRIES

PREP TIME: **10 MINUTES**

COOK TIME: **3 MINUTES**

DIFFICULTY: **MEDIUM**

SERVES: **2**

VEGGIE

Bless yourself with these crunchy, tangy, sensational halloumi fries... Look out for that chilli KICK.

INGREDIENTS

2 x 250 g (9 oz) blocks of halloumi cheese

60 g (2¼ oz) hot chilli–flavoured tortilla chips

75 g (2¾ oz) plain flour

2 eggs, lightly beaten

500 ml (18 fl oz) vegetable oil, for deep-frying

METHOD

1. Pat dry the blocks of halloumi with kitchen paper and slice into chunky fries. You should get 6 fries from each block.

2. Using a rolling pin, the base of a heavy jar or a mortar, crush the tortilla chips to a fine crumb. Tip into a shallow bowl.

3. Put the flour in a second shallow bowl and the eggs in a third.

4. Coat the halloumi fries in the flour, followed by the egg and finally the tortilla–chip crumb. Lay the coated fries on a plate.

5. Heat the oil, in a deep saucepan with a well–fitting lid (see page 17), to 180°C (350°F) and fry the halloumi fries for 2½ minutes, until crisp and golden on the outside and melting in the middle. You may wish to do this in batches to avoid overcrowding the pan. Remove and drain on kitchen paper before serving.

CHILLI-CHEESE GARLIC BREAD

TRUST US! This chilli-cheese garlic bread will elevate the vibes on the dinner table and spice up your night for sure.

INGREDIENTS

1 large garlic bulb

1 tablespoon olive oil

100 g (3½ oz) salted butter, softened

2 tablespoons chopped parsley leaves

1 tablespoon red chilli paste

1 large ciabatta loaf, about 270g (9¾ oz)

100 g (3½ oz) grated mozzarella cheese

salt and pepper

METHOD

1. Preheat the oven to 200°C (400°F), Gas Mark 6.

2. Slice the top off the bulb of garlic then drizzle the bulb with the olive oil and season with a pinch each of salt and pepper. Wrap in kitchen foil and bake for 30 minutes until soft in the middle. Leave the oven on.

3. In a bowl, combine the softened butter with the parsley, red chilli paste and the roasted garlic cloves, squeezed from their skins. Mix with a fork until well combined.

4. Slice the ciabatta in half lengthways and score each half in a grid pattern. Spread generously with the spicy garlic butter and top with the grated mozzarella.

5. Bake for 15 minutes until crisp and bubbling.

Elevate the vibes on the dinner table

ICE-CUBE PIZZA BITES

PREP TIME: **20 MINUTES**
COOK TIME: **12 MINUTES**
DIFFICULTY: **EASY**
SERVES: **3**
VEGAN

For our pizza fans, this ice-cube hack will change your life, trust me! Mini deep-pan pizzas oozing with flavour.

INGREDIENTS

400 g (14 oz) packet of pre-rolled pizza dough or vegan shortcrust pastry

60 g (2¼ oz) sun-dried tomatoes, chopped

40 g (1½ oz) grated vegan cheese

12 teaspoons vegan tomato pizza sauce (or see page 15)

30 g (1 oz) plain flour, to dust

2 tablespoons olive oil

1 tablespoon Italian mixed dried herbs

METHOD

1. Preheat the oven to 200°C (400°F), Gas Mark 6 and line a baking tray with nonstick baking paper.

2. Slice the sheet of pizza dough or pastry in half widthways, so you have 2 smaller rectangular sheets. Place 1 sheet over an ice-cube tray and gently push down into the individual moulds, without breaking the sheet.

3. Divide the sun-dried tomatoes between the moulds, then the vegan cheese, then add 1 teaspoon of pizza sauce to each mould (ice-cube trays generally have 12 moulds).

4. Brush water over the dough or pastry at the edges of the cubes and lay the second sheet over the top, pressing it down to seal the edges.

5. Dust a worktop with the flour and turn over the ice-cube tray to turn out the contents. Use a knife or pizza cutter to slice into individual bites.

6. Arrange the bites across the prepared baking tray, brush with the olive oil and top with the dried herbs. Bake for 12 minutes and serve.

SIZZLIN' OVEN-BAKED PIZZA DIP

PREP TIME: **5 MINUTES**
COOK TIME: **15 MINUTES**
DIFFICULTY: **EASY**
SERVES: **2**
VEGGIE

This recipe is IT: bubbling burrata with tangy pizza sauce IN DIP FORM. Flavours on flavours. Don't say we don't spoil you. No more basic hummus for you after you try this, G.

INGREDIENTS

250 ml (9 fl oz) tomato pizza sauce (or see page 15)

150 g (5½ oz) ball of Italian burrata, or mozzarella

1 garlic clove, crushed

1 tablespoon olive oil

¼ teaspoon chilli flakes

salt and pepper

small handful of basil leaves

2–4 slices of baked garlic bread, ideally Chilli–Cheese Garlic Bread (see page 20), to serve

METHOD

1. Preheat the oven to 200°C (400°F), Gas Mark 6.

2. Pour the tomato sauce into a small ovenproof dish and place the burrata in the centre.

3. In a small bowl, combine the crushed garlic with the olive oil, chilli flakes and salt and pepper, then drizzle this over the dish.

4. Bake for 15 minutes until golden, molten and bubbling.

5. Sprinkle with basil and serve with the garlic bread for dipping.

SALT & PEPPER SQUID

PREP TIME: **10 MINUTES**
COOK TIME: **5 MINUTES**
DIFFICULTY: **EASY**
SERVES: **2**
FISH

This salt and pepps squid is so cute and crispy it's DANGEROUS. Best know we're gonna eat 40 without realising...

INGREDIENTS

200 g (7 oz) frozen raw squid tubes, or squid rings
50 g (1¾ oz) cornflour
200 ml (7 fl oz) vegetable oil
1 teaspoon chilli powder
¼ teaspoon sea salt
¼ teaspoon ground black pepper
lime wedges, to serve
sweet chilli sauce, for dipping

METHOD

1. Defrost the squid according to the packet instructions.

2. Slice the squid tubes, if using, into rings, roughly 2 cm (¾ inch) wide. Pat the squid dry with kitchen paper.

3. Put the cornflour into a shallow bowl. Toss the squid in the cornflour.

4. Heat the oil in a frying pan over a medium–high heat and shallow–fry the squid for 2 minutes, turning halfway, until curled up, crisp and pale golden. (You may have to cook them in 2 batches, depending on the size of the pan.) Remove the squid pieces and drain on kitchen paper.

5. Combine the chilli powder, salt and pepper in a medium–sized bowl and toss through the fried squid pieces, ensuring they are evenly coated in the seasoning.

6. Serve with lime wedges to squeeze and your favourite sweet chilli dipping sauce.

TIP:
You can find frozen squid tubes, or squid rings, in the frozen section of larger supermarkets.

CHEESY POPCORN

The controversy over this dish is mad, but don't hate us. TRY IT FIRST! Movie-night vibes all over this snack.

INGREDIENTS

30 g (1 oz) unsalted butter

1 teaspoon yeast extract spread, such as Marmite

30 g (1 oz) finely grated Cheddar cheese

2 tablespoons vegetable oil

75 g (2¾ oz) popcorn kernels

METHOD

1. Preheat the oven to 160°C (350°F), Gas Mark 3. Line a baking sheet with nonstick baking paper.

2. Melt the butter in a small saucepan over a low heat. Stir in the yeast extract and grated Cheddar until well combined and smooth. Remove from the heat and set aside.

3. Heat the oil in a large, deep saucepan with a well-fitting lid set over a medium-high heat. Add the popcorn kernels. Cover with the lid and give the pan a shake to ensure that the kernels are coated in the oil.

4. Shake the pan every minute or so. After a couple of minutes, the kernels will start to pop. Do not remove the lid.

5. Once the kernels are popping at a rapid pace, remove the pan from the heat and continue to shake every minute, but do not remove the lid until the popping has stopped.

6. When it is safe to remove the lid, stir in the cheesy butter, ensuring the popcorn is evenly coated.

7. Tip the cheesy popcorn on to the prepared baking sheet, bake for 5 minutes until perfectly crisp and enjoy.

GARLIC & PARMESAN POTATO WEDGES

PREP TIME: **10 MINUTES**

COOK TIME: **1 HOUR**

DIFFICULTY: **EASY**

SERVES: **2**

VEGGIE

Don't be shook by the whole garlic bulb, as roasting makes it sweet and caramelised: these cheesy herby garlicky wedges are BANGING!

INGREDIENTS

1 large garlic bulb

4 tablespoons olive oil

3 large baking potatoes, sliced into thick wedges

2 teaspoons fresh thyme leaves

3 tablespoons finely grated vegetarian Parmesan cheese

salt and pepper

your favourite dips, to serve

METHOD

1. Preheat the oven to 200°C (400°F), Gas Mark 6.

2. Slice the top off the bulb of garlic, then drizzle the bulb with 1 tablespoon of the oil and season with a pinch each of salt and pepper. Wrap the bulb in kitchen foil and bake for 30 minutes until soft in the centre.

3. Meanwhile, arrange the potato wedges across a large baking tray.

4. Once cooked, squeeze the soft garlic cloves into a small bowl, discarding the skins. Combine with the remaining olive oil, half of the thyme leaves and 2 tablespoons of the grated Parmesan.

5. Drizzle the cheesy garlic oil over the potato wedges and massage it in with your hands, ensuring the wedges are well coated.

6. Bake for 30 minutes, turning halfway, until crisp and golden. Sprinkle with the remaining thyme leaves and Parmesan and serve with your favourite dips.

SHROOM WINGS

These golden, crispy, meaty mushroom wings will leave you discombobulated when you realise they're VEGAN.

INGREDIENTS

150 g (5½ oz) plain flour

2 teaspoons smoked paprika

2 teaspoons Italian mixed dried herbs

1 teaspoon salt

2 teaspoons onion powder

2 teaspoons garlic powder

200 ml (7 fl oz) plant-based milk

180 g (6 oz) golden breadcrumbs

300 g (10½ oz) baby portobello mushrooms, stalks removed, halved

1 litre (1¾ pints) vegetable oil, for deep-frying

vegan barbecue-style sauce, for dipping

METHOD

1. In a large mixing bowl, combine the flour, smoked paprika, dried herbs, salt, onion powder, garlic powder and plant-based milk. Whisk this batter until it is thick and smooth.

2. Put the breadcrumbs into a medium-sized bowl.

3. Coat the mushroom halves in the batter, followed by the breadcrumbs, and lay across a plate or wire rack.

4. Heat the oil, in a deep saucepan with a well-fitting lid, to 180°C (350°F) over a low-medium heat. (See page 17 for deep-frying hacks.)

5. Fry the 'wings' in batches for 3 minutes, or until golden and crisp. Remove from the oil and drain on a few sheets of kitchen paper. Serve with your favourite vegan barbecue-style sauce.

TIP:

Want to make your own golden breadcrumbs? See our hack on page 88.

PRAWN TOAST ROLL-UPS

PREP TIME: **20 MINUTES**
COOK TIME: **12 MINUTES**
DIFFICULTY: **EASY**
SERVES: **4**
FISH

**Crispy, crunchy and all-round VIBES!
I'm tucking these juicy prawns into their
toasty bread-bed and they're getting
munched immediately.**

INGREDIENTS

170 g (6 oz) raw king prawns

1 teaspoon salt

1 teaspoon ground white pepper

1 teaspoon ground ginger

1 teaspoon soy sauce

3 eggs, 1 separated

12 white bread slices

4 tablespoons white sesame seeds

2 tablespoons black sesame seeds

3 tablespoons unsalted butter

sweet chilli sauce, for dipping

METHOD

1. Put the prawns, salt, white pepper, ginger, soy sauce and egg white in a food processor or high-powered blender and blend to a smooth paste. Cover and place in the refrigerator until needed.

2. Stack the slices of bread on a board and slice off the crusts. Make breadcrumbs with those, for use at a later date (see page 88).

3. Use a rolling pin to flatten a slice of bread, then evenly spread it with 1½ teaspoons of the prawn paste. Combine the white and black sesame seeds in a small bowl, sprinkle a small pinch over the top of the bread slice, then roll it up tightly into a cigar. Repeat to flatten, fill and roll all the bread slices.

4. Whisk the remaining eggs and egg yolk in a shallow bowl. Dip the roll-ups in the egg, turning to coat, then scatter over the remaining sesame seeds.

5. Melt the butter in a frying pan over a low-medium heat and fry the prawn toast roll-ups for 10-12 minutes, turning regularly, until evenly golden. Serve with sweet chilli dipping sauce.

CANDIED TWIST BACON

Have you ever heard the phrase 'don't get your bacon in a twist?' No, us neither, but these crispy candied bacon twists SLAP!

INGREDIENTS

220 g (8 oz) streaky bacon rashers
1 teaspoon light brown sugar
½ teaspoon cayenne pepper

METHOD

1. Preheat the oven to 200°C (400°F), Gas Mark 6. Line a baking tray with kitchen foil.

2. Twist the bacon rashers into tight ringlets and arrange them lengthways across the prepared baking tray.

3. Combine the light brown sugar and cayenne pepper in a small bowl and sprinkle this over the bacon twists.

4. Bake for 35 minutes, until golden and crisp. (It takes this long for them to cook as they are tightly twisted.)

5. Remove the twists from the oven and place on some kitchen paper to drain off any excess fat. Serve with tomato ketchup or brown sauce, add to your next Full English (see page 71) or go double-bacon *and* dip into a soft-boiled egg yolk with our Bacon Egg Cups (see page 76).

TIP:
To elevate your twists, wrap the bacon around cheese strings and enjoy these stretchy treats!

RED-HOT POPCORN CHICKEN

PREP TIME: **15 MINUTES**
COOK TIME: **15 MINUTES**
DIFFICULTY: **MEDIUM**
SERVES: **2**
MEAT

**Crispy, spicy and fierce finger food
for all the gang at the shubz.**

INGREDIENTS

70 g (2½ oz) hot chilli-flavoured corn
   puffs, crushed to a fine crumb

50 g (1¾ oz) plain flour

½ teaspoon cayenne pepper

½ teaspoon smoked paprika

¼ teaspoon garlic powder

¼ teaspoon salt

1 egg

2 chicken breasts, chopped into
   2.5 cm (1 inch) cubes

500 ml (18 fl oz) vegetable oil,
   for deep-frying (optional)

Buffalo sauce, for dipping

METHOD

1. If baking the chicken, preheat the oven to 180°C (350°F), Gas Mark 4.

2. Using a rolling pin, the base of a heavy jar or a mortar, gently crush
    the corn puffs to a fine crumb. Tip the crumb into a bowl.

3. In another bowl, combine the flour, cayenne pepper, smoked paprika,
    garlic powder and salt. Lightly beat the egg in a third bowl.

4. Toss the chicken through the seasoned flour, ensuring it is well coated.
    Next, turn the pieces in the egg, followed by the corn-puff crumb.

5. If deep-frying, heat the oil, in a deep saucepan with a well-fitting lid,
    to 180°C (350°F) over a low-medium heat. Once the oil reaches this
    temperature, reduce the heat to low. Fry the chicken in batches for
    3½ minutes until evenly golden. Remove from the oil and drain on a
    couple of sheets of kitchen paper. Let the chicken cool for at least
    5 minutes before tucking in. (See page 17 for deep-frying hacks.)

6. Alternatively, bake the popcorn chicken in the preheated oven, on
    a wire rack set over an oven tray, for 15 minutes.

7. Serve with Buffalo sauce, for dipping.

TORTILLA CHIPS

3

WAYS

Whether you're feeling sweet, savoury or spicy, we got you. What's our favourite of the three? Pass.

CINNAMON SUGAR

PREP TIME: **5 MINUTES**
COOK TIME: **5 MINUTES**
DIFFICULTY: **EASY**
SERVES: **2**
VEGGIE

INGREDIENTS

1 teaspoon caster sugar

½ teaspoon ground cinnamon

3 small flour tortillas

30 g (1 oz) salted butter, melted

3 tablespoons chocolate and hazelnut spread, such as Nutella, melted

METHOD

1. Preheat the oven to 160°C (325°F), Gas Mark 3. Line a baking tray with nonstick baking paper.

2. Combine the caster sugar and cinnamon in a small bowl.

3. Pile up the tortillas on a board and slice into 8 even wedges, making 24 chips.

4. Lay out the tortilla chips across the prepared tray and brush with the melted butter.

5. Sprinkle with the cinnamon sugar and bake for 5–6 minutes until golden and crisp.

6. Serve with the melted chocolate and hazelnut spread, for dipping.

SMOKIN'

PREP TIME: **5 MINUTES**
COOK TIME: **5 MINUTES**
DIFFICULTY: **EASY**
SERVES: **4**
VEGAN

INGREDIENTS

1 teaspoon smoked paprika
½ teaspoon cayenne pepper
¼ teaspoon salt
3 small flour tortillas
1 tablespoon olive oil
salsa, to serve (optional)

METHOD

1. Preheat the oven to 160°C (325°F), Gas Mark 3. Line a baking tray with nonstick baking paper.

2. Combine the smoked paprika, cayenne pepper and salt in a small bowl.

3. Pile up the tortillas on a board and slice into 8 even wedges, making 24 chips.

4. Lay out the tortilla chips across the prepared tray and brush with the olive oil.

5. Sprinkle with the spice mix and bake for 5–6 minutes until golden and crisp.

6. Serve with salsa, for dipping, if you like.

GARLIC CHEESE

PREP TIME: **10 MINUTES**
COOK TIME: **5 MINUTES**
DIFFICULTY: **EASY**
SERVES: **4**
VEGGIE

INGREDIENTS

1 teaspoon garlic powder
2 teaspoons Italian mixed dried herbs
2 tablespoons finely grated vegetarian Parmesan cheese, or Grana Padano cheese
3 small flour tortillas
2 tablespoons olive oil
pinch of salt
guacamole, to serve (optional)

METHOD

1. Preheat the oven to 160°C (325°F), Gas Mark 3. Line a baking tray with nonstick baking paper.

2. Combine the garlic powder, Italian herbs, cheese and a pinch of salt in a small bowl.

3. Pile up the tortillas on a board and slice the pile into 8 even wedges, making 24 chips.

4. Lay out the tortilla chips across the prepared tray and brush with the olive oil.

5. Sprinkle with the garlic and cheese mixture and bake in the oven for 5–6 minutes until golden and crisp.

6. Serve with guacamole, for dipping, if you like.

GARLIC CHEESE

CINNAMON SUGAR

CANDY SHOP CHOCOLATE BARK

We're taking indulgence to a whole new level with a mash-up of nostalgic sweeties. Keep chewing for them explosions of popping candy!

INGREDIENTS

200 g (7 oz) white chocolate chips
200 g (7 oz) milk chocolate chips
handful of salted pretzels
handful of jelly beans
7 g (¼ oz) sachet of popping candy
38 g (1½ oz) tube of multicoloured, sugar–coated chocolate sweets
15 g (½ oz) flaky milk chocolate bar, broken into pieces

METHOD

1. Melt the white chocolate and milk chocolate separately in heatproof bowls, each set over a saucepan of gently simmering water.

2. Line a large baking tray with nonstick baking paper and pour over the melted milk chocolate. Using a spatula, spread the chocolate out into a rectangle, about 30 x 20 cm (12 x 8 inches).

3. Spoon over the melted white chocolate, ensuring you leave space between each spoonful so you can see the contrast between the milk and white chocolate. Swirl a toothpick or skewer through the chocolate to create a marbling effect.

4. Scatter over the remaining ingredients for a colourful and textured chocolate bark, then transfer to the refrigerator for 30 minutes to set.

5. Roughly chop into bite–sized pieces to serve.

CHURROS BITES

PREP TIME: **10 MINUTES**
COOK TIME: **15–20 MINUTES**
DIFFICULTY: **MEDIUM**
SERVES: **4**
VEGGIE

These fluffy and sugary churros finessed with a melted chocolate dip will make your heart sing, G – trust me.

INGREDIENTS

250 ml (9 fl oz) water

50 g (1¾ oz) unsalted butter, cubed

55 g (2 oz) caster sugar

¼ teaspoon salt

250 g (9 oz) plain flour

¼ teaspoon bicarbonate of soda

1 litre (1¾ pints) vegetable oil, for deep–frying

½ teaspoon ground cinnamon

melted chocolate, to serve (optional)

METHOD

1. In a saucepan, combine the measured water, butter, 2 teaspoons of the caster sugar and the salt. Place over a low heat to allow the butter to melt, then take off the heat.

2. Sift the flour and bicarbonate of soda into a large mixing bowl and make a well in the centre. Pour in the melted butter mixture and beat, quickly, with a wooden spoon, until you have a smooth, thick dough.

3. Spoon the dough into a piping bag fitted with a large star–shaped piping nozzle and set aside.

4. Heat the oil, in a deep saucepan with a well–fitting lid, to 180°C (350°F) over a low-medium heat. Line a plate with kitchen paper and place this near the saucepan. (See page 17 for deep–frying hacks.)

5. Carefully pipe the dough into the oil, using kitchen scissors to cut it into 2.5-5 cm (1-2 inch) churros as you pipe. Fry the churros in batches for 5-6 minutes until golden and crisp. Remove from the oil with a slotted spoon and drain on the prepared plate.

6. Mix the remaining caster sugar with the ground cinnamon in a shallow bowl and roll the churros in it, ensuring they are well coated. Serve with a small bowl of melted chocolate for dipping, if you like.

PREP TIME: **5 MINUTES**

COOK TIME: **15 MINUTES**

DIFFICULTY: **MEDIUM**

SERVES: **4**

VEGAN

DIY HONEYCOMB

You know them ones where you're craving a sweet treat but don't wanna leave the house? This is a four-ingredient store-cupboard winner for lazy nights in.

INGREDIENTS

200 g (7 oz) caster sugar

75 g (2¾ oz) golden syrup

1 tablespoon water

1 tablespoon bicarbonate of soda

METHOD

1. Line a 20-cm (8-inch) square baking tin with nonstick baking paper.

2. Put the caster sugar, golden syrup and water into a large saucepan and gently melt over a low heat. This should take about 10 minutes.

3. When the sugar has completely melted, increase the temperature to a low-medium heat and gently simmer for 5 minutes, or until the mixture turns a pale amber colour.

4. Remove from the heat and sift in the bicarbonate of soda, then stir the mixture vigorously with a wooden spoon until the bicarbonate of soda is fully incorporated. It will foam up and expand quite rapidly.

5. Transfer the mixture to the prepared baking tin and set aside for about 30 minutes to cool and harden.

6. Once the honeycomb is set, turn it out of the tin, peel away the baking paper, then break into bite-sized pieces. Delicious on its own, dipped into melted chocolate and left to set, or crumbled over ice cream.

CAUGHT BRUNCHIN'

CAUGHT'S TOP EGG-COOKING HACKS

These eggcellent hacks are no yolk. Absolute cracking tips 'n' tricks from yours truly. Don't say we don't spoil you lot.

EGG SEPARATION HACK

PREP TIME: **1 MINUTE**

COOK TIME: **NONE**

DIFFICULTY: **EASY**

SERVES: **1**

VEGGIE

INGREDIENTS

1 egg

METHOD

1. Crack the egg into a small bowl.

2. Remove the lid from a clean, empty plastic bottle and gently squeeze the sides of the bottle. Hold the opening over the egg yolk and release your pressure on the bottle. The yolk will get sucked into the bottle opening, separating it from the white.

3. Squeeze the bottle to release the yolk into a separate bowl or container.

EGG POCKET HACK

PREP TIME: **1 MINUTE**

COOK TIME: **5 MINUTES**

DIFFICULTY: **EASY**

SERVES: **1**

VEGGIE

INGREDIENTS

½ tablespoon vegetable oil

1 egg

METHOD

1. Heat the oil in a frying pan over a medium heat.

2. Separate the egg white from the yolk (using the Egg Seperation Hack shown opposite) and add the white to the pan. Swirl the pan to ensure that the egg white is evenly distributed.

3. Once the egg white is cooked through, gently tip the yolk into the centre of the egg white and fold over the sides, sealing the yolk into a neat pocket. Cook for 1 minute, then flip and cook for a further minute.

4. Serve on buttered toast, cutting into the pocket for that runny yolk deliciousness!

LADLE POACHED EGGS

PREP TIME: **NONE**

COOK TIME: **6 MINUTES**

DIFFICULTY: **EASY**

SERVES: **1**

VEGGIE

INGREDIENTS

½ teaspoon vegetable oil

1 egg

METHOD

1. Bring a small saucepan of water to the boil.

2. Lightly oil a stainless–steel ladle with the oil and crack the egg into it. Lower the ladle into the boiling water so that the water comes up the sides but doesn't overflow on to the egg.

3. Hold the ladle in the simmering water for 4–6 minutes, or until cooked through.

4. Serve on toast with seasoned avocado, chilli flakes and salt and pepper, if you like.

MICROWAVE 'BAKED' EGGS

PREP TIME: **1 MINUTE**

COOK TIME: **1½–2 MINUTES**

DIFFICULTY: **EASY**

SERVES: **1**

VEGGIE

INGREDIENTS

½ teaspoon vegetable oil

1 egg

salt and pepper

METHOD

1. Oil the inside of a mug with the vegetable oil and crack in the egg. Season with salt and pepper and microwave on high for 1½–2 minutes until the egg is cooked through.

2. Run a cutlery knife around the edge of the egg to release it from the mug and serve on toast.

3. You could also try putting mashed avocado, baked beans or grated cheese in the mug before cracking the egg over. Microwave on high for 1½–2 minutes and enjoy straight out of the mug.

MICROWAVE 'POACHED' EGGS

PREP TIME: **1 MINUTES**

COOK TIME: **1½ MINUTES**

DIFFICULTY: **EASY**

SERVES: **1**

VEGGIE

INGREDIENTS

1 teaspoon white wine vinegar

1 egg

METHOD

1. Fill a mug with boiling water and add the vinegar. Crack the egg into the mug and microwave on high for 1½ minutes.

2. Drain the egg and serve on buttered toast, with avocado, if you like.

STRIPEY
CHEESE OMELETTE

PREP TIME: **1 MINUTE**   COOK TIME: **10 MINUTES**

DIFFICULTY: **EASY**   SERVES: **1**

VEGGIE

INGREDIENTS

3 eggs

1 teaspoon unsalted butter

25 g (1 oz) grated Cheddar cheese

salt and pepper

METHOD

1. Separate the eggs (see page 52) and melt the butter in a large frying pan over a medium heat.

2. Whisk the yolks and pour them into the pan, swirling them so they are evenly distributed across the base of the pan. Cook for about 1 minute, until set, then remove the pan from the heat.

3. Using a small, sharp knife, cut vertical lines in the yolk so that you have strips roughly 2cm (¾ inch) wide. Carefully peel away every other strip of egg yolk (eating it as you go).

4. Return the pan to the heat and pour over the egg whites. As the whites cook, they will fill the gaps in the yolk, leaving distinct stripes.

5. When the egg whites are almost set, sprinkle over the Cheddar and season with salt and pepper. Fold in each side of the omelette to cover the filling. Cook for about 30 seconds, then slide a spatula underneath and quickly flip. Cook for a further 30 seconds until the cheese is melty.

6. Serve immediately and enjoy this sensational breakfast!

These eggcellent hacks are no yolk

SHAKEN UP 'SHAKSHUKA'

PREP TIME: **10 MINUTES**

COOK TIME: **25 MINUTES**

DIFFICULTY: **EASY**

SERVES: **4**

VEGGIE

As if one pesto isn't enough, we went in with the red AND green. Why? You know why. This shakshuka will shake up everyone at the shubz, trust us.

INGREDIENTS

1 tablespoon olive oil

1 onion, finely chopped

4 tablespoons vegetarian red pesto

2 x 400 g (14 oz) cans of chopped tomatoes

4 eggs

2 avocados, sliced

100 g (3½ oz) feta or goats' cheese, crumbled

small pinch of chilli flakes

2 tablespoons vegetarian green pesto

crusty garlic bread, to serve (optional, for homemade see page 20)

METHOD

1. Heat the olive oil in a large, deep frying pan with a well–fitting lid over a medium heat.

2. Reduce the heat to low-medium and sweat the onion for 5 minutes, until starting to turn translucent.

3. Add the red pesto and chopped tomatoes and stir to combine. Bring to a simmer and cook for 10 minutes to thicken the sauce.

4. Use a spoon to create 4 wells in the sauce and crack in the eggs. Top the shakshuka with the sliced avocado, crumbled cheese and chilli flakes, then cover and simmer for a further 10 minutes, or until the eggs are cooked through.

5. Add a few dollops of green pesto and serve with crusty garlic bread for dipping, if you like.

SMOKY SALMON & POTATO MUFFINS

Don't get it twisted, muffins can be savoury too, you know? Smoky salmon, 'cause we fancy, finessed with good flavours. Why not indulge in a muffin first thing in the AM?

INGREDIENTS

6 eggs, lightly beaten

2 tablespoons milk

1 large Maris Piper potato, peeled and chopped into 1 cm (½–inch) cubes

150 g (5½ oz) hot–smoked salmon, torn into chunks

2 teaspoons finely chopped chives, plus extra to serve

¼ teaspoon salt

¼ teaspoon cracked black pepper

3 teaspoons olive oil

METHOD

1. Preheat the oven to 180°C (350°F), Gas Mark 4 and line a muffin tray with 8 paper cases.

2. Combine the eggs and milk in a large bowl, then add the potato, salmon, chives, salt and pepper.

3. Distribute the mixture evenly between the muffin cases. Bake for 20-25 minutes until golden and risen. Sprinkle with more chives and serve immediately. Alternatively, wait until cooled and then store in an airtight container in the refrigerator (to keep the fish fresh) for up to 2 days.

TIP:
You can make these the day before, then eat them chilled or warmed through in the oven.

FIVE-MINUTE MICROWAVE EGGS ROYALE

PREP TIME: **5 MINUTES**
COOK TIME: **5 MINUTES**
DIFFICULTY: **EASY**
SERVES: **2**
FISH

Do you want to be classy? But only have 5 minutes before you need to leave? NO STRESS G, this tasty hollandaise egg hack will get you out the door with happy taste buds and sophistication.

INGREDIENTS

60 g (2¼ oz) unsalted butter

6 eggs

60 ml (4 tablespoons) double cream

1 lemon, cut into 4 wedges

¼ teaspoon salt

pinch of black pepper

4 teaspoons white wine vinegar

4 English muffins, toasted and buttered

100 g (3½ oz) smoked salmon or trout

cayenne pepper

METHOD

1. Place the butter into a medium bowl and microwave on high for 30 seconds until melted.

2. Separate 2 of the eggs, reserving the egg whites for another recipe.

3. In a small bowl, whisk together the 2 egg yolks with the double cream, juice from one of the lemon wedges, and salt and pepper. Pour the egg mixture into the melted butter and whisk until well combined.

4. Return to the microwave for 1–2 minutes, stopping every 15 seconds to whisk the mixture. This hollandaise sauce is ready once it has thickened to a creamy, custard–like consistency. Cover and set aside.

5. Fill 4 mugs with boiling water and add 1 teaspoon of the vinegar to each. Crack an egg into each mug and microwave, 2 mugs at a time, on high for 1½ minutes.

6. Meanwhile, top the muffins with the salmon or trout. Drain the eggs and serve on the muffins, topped with the hollandaise, a pinch of cayenne pepper and the remaining lemon wedges on the side for squeezing over.

PREP TIME: **5 MINUTES**
COOK TIME: **20 MINUTES**
DIFFICULTY: **EASY**
SERVES: **2**
VEGGIE

COOKIE DOUGH BAKED OATS

No better start to your day than these BANGING cookie dough oats! The sugar kick be real.

INGREDIENTS

1 banana

100 g (3½ oz) oatmeal, or substitute regular porridge oats blended in a food processor

2 tablespoons runny honey

1 tablespoon smooth peanut butter (optional)

½ teaspoon baking powder

¼ teaspoon salt

120 ml (4 fl oz) milk (dairy or plant-based)

50 g (1¾ oz) chocolate chips

METHOD

1. Preheat the oven to 180°C (350°F), Gas Mark 4.

2. Mash the banana with a fork in a medium bowl, then add the oatmeal, runny honey, smooth peanut butter (if using), baking powder, salt, milk and half the chocolate chips. Stir to combine, then tip into 2 small ovenproof ramekins.

3. Top with the remaining chocolate chips and bake for 20 minutes until risen and golden. Serve straight away.

PILE-UP POTATO NACHOS

PREP TIME: **15 MINUTES**

COOK TIME: **30–40 MINUTES**

DIFFICULTY: **EASY**

SERVES: **4**

VEGAN

Hear us out: swap tortilla chips for crispy potato slices and load up with black beans, spicy jalapeños and, of course, BARE cheese and avo. You won't be disappointed with this one.

INGREDIENTS

8 Maris Piper, King Edward or sweet potatoes, finely sliced

3 tablespoons olive oil

2 teaspoons smoked paprika

¼ teaspoon salt

200 g (7 oz) grated vegan cheese

400 g (14 oz) can of black beans, drained

2 avocados, sliced

2 jalapeños, sliced

80 g (2¾ oz) vegan yogurt (optional)

To serve (all optional)

coriander

lime wedges

METHOD

1. Preheat the oven to 190°C (375°F), Gas Mark 5. Line a baking tray with nonstick baking paper and set aside for later.

2. In a large bowl, toss the potato slices in the oil, smoked paprika and salt.

3. Lay the potato slices across 1–2 baking trays and bake for 20–25 minutes, or until golden and starting to crisp up.

4. Once cooked, pile half the potato nachos on to the prepared baking tray. Top with half the grated cheese, half the black beans, half the avocados and half the jalapeños.

5. Layer over the rest of the potato nachos and top with the remaining cheese, beans, avocados and jalapeños. Return to the oven for 10–15 minutes until everything is warmed through and the cheese is melted.

6. Serve on the tray, or transfer to a serving platter and top with dollops of yogurt. Scatter with coriander and lime wedges, if you like.

CROQUE MADAME CROISSANT BAKE

PREP TIME: **10 MINUTES**
COOK TIME: **15 MINUTES**
DIFFICULTY: **EASY**
SERVES: **4**
MEAT

This dish tastes banging and is a sick way to turn it up when sharing with the mandem. Fill croissants with honey-roast ham and cheese, cover with creamy sauce, bake 'til bubblin' and whack a crispy fried egg on top... OOOOFT.

INGREDIENTS

4 croissants

4 thick slices of honey–roast ham

100 g (3½ oz) grated Cheddar cheese

6 eggs

20 ml (4 teaspoons) double cream

100 ml (3½ fl oz) whole milk

¼ teaspoon salt

¼ teaspoon cracked black pepper

knob of salted butter

METHOD

1. Preheat the oven to 180°C (350°F), Gas Mark 4.

2. Slice the croissants in half and fill with the slices of ham and half the cheese. Arrange the filled croissants on a baking tray with a shallow lip.

3. Lightly beat 2 of the eggs in a medium–sized bowl, then stir in the double cream, whole milk, remaining Cheddar and salt and pepper.

4. Pour the egg mixture over the croissants and bake for 12 minutes until the cheese is melted and bubbling.

5. Meanwhile, melt the butter in a large frying pan over a medium–high heat and fry the remaining 4 eggs.

6. Remove the croissant bake from the oven and serve straight away, with each portion topped with a crispy fried egg.

FROSTED-FLAKE CHICKEN WAFFLES

Just PREE the marriage between sweet and savoury, flavours made in holy matrimony. Don't ask questions, make this sensational frosted-flake chicken and waffles and thank us later.

INGREDIENTS

300 ml (½ pint) buttermilk

2 tablespoons hot sauce

1 teaspoon garlic powder

2 chicken breasts, each cut into 6 strips

300 g (10½ oz) frosted flakes

4 shop-bought Belgian waffles

salt

maple syrup, to serve

METHOD

1. Combine the buttermilk, hot sauce, garlic powder and a large pinch of salt in a medium-sized bowl.

2. Add the chicken to the seasoned buttermilk, ensuring the strips are well coated. Cover and allow to marinate in the refrigerator for 1 hour or, ideally, overnight.

3. Preheat the oven to 200°C (400°F), Gas Mark 6.

4. Gather the frosted flakes inside a clean tea towel and use a rolling pin to gently roll and bash the flakes to a fine crumb.

5. Coat the marinated chicken strips in the frosted-flake crumb and place on a wire rack set over an oven tray. Bake for 30 minutes, or until golden brown, flipping halfway.

6. Heat the waffles according to the packet instructions.

7. Stack the chicken on the waffles and serve, drizzled generously with maple syrup.

ONE-TRAY FULL ENGLISH

PREP TIME: **5 MINUTES**
COOK TIME: **40 MINUTES**
DIFFICULTY: **EASY**
SERVES: **4**
MEAT

Forget pots and pans: the Full English is a one-tray ting from now onwards. Get stuck in with the big boi with all the British breakfast staples! Do not think of skipping the buttered toast or the red or brown sauce on the side.

INGREDIENTS

4 bacon rashers

4 pork sausages

8 shop-bought hash browns

200 g (7 oz) chestnut mushrooms, quartered

10 cherry tomatoes

200 g (7 oz) canned baked beans

4 eggs

handful of parsley leaves, roughly chopped, optional

buttered toast, to serve

METHOD

1. Preheat the oven to 200°C (400°F), Gas Mark 6.

2. Arrange the bacon rashers, sausages, hash browns, mushrooms and cherry tomatoes across a large oven tray. Add the baked beans in large spoonfuls, spaced out across the tray.

3. Transfer to the oven for 30 minutes or until the vegetables are tender and the sausages are golden brown and cooked through.

4. Remove the tray from the oven and make 4 wells with a spoon. Crack the eggs into the wells and return to the oven for 10 minutes, or until the egg whites are firm.

5. Sprinkle with chopped parsley (if using) and serve with buttery toast and your favourite breakfast sauce.

PANCAKE CEREAL

Mini fluffy pancakes, marshmallows and cookies floating in chocolate milk? Best believe it, 'cos we went there. A sugary sweet start to your day for them ones when muesli isn't an option.

INGREDIENTS

1 egg

125 g (4½ oz) plain flour

150 ml (¼ pint) whole milk

1 teaspoon golden syrup

2 tablespoons mini marshmallows (optional)

1 tablespoon mini cookies (optional)

chocolate milk, to serve

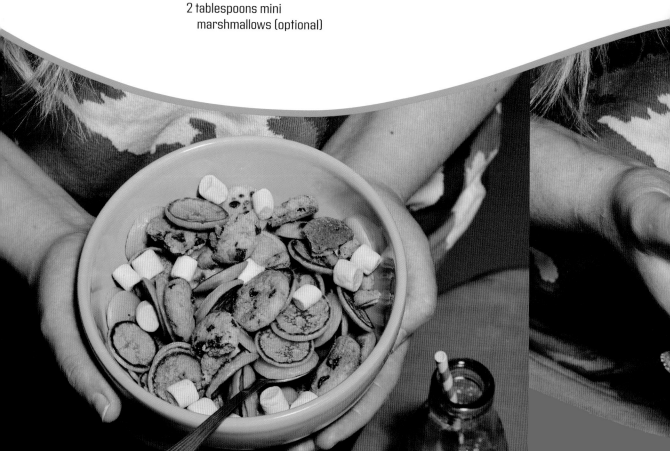

METHOD

1. In a bowl, beat the egg, flour, milk and golden syrup into a smooth batter and pour it into a squeezy sauce bottle fitted with a nozzle.

2. Heat a nonstick frying pan over a medium heat.

3. Pipe some of the batter into the pan, in rounds about 2 cm (¾ inch) wide. Cook for 20 seconds on each side, flipping with a butter knife, until evenly golden. You will have to repeat this process 3–4 times to use up all the batter.

4. Allow the pancakes to cool on a piece of kitchen paper, then put them in a cereal bowl. Scatter with the mini marshmallows and mini cookies for added texture, if you like.

5. Serve with chocolate milk.

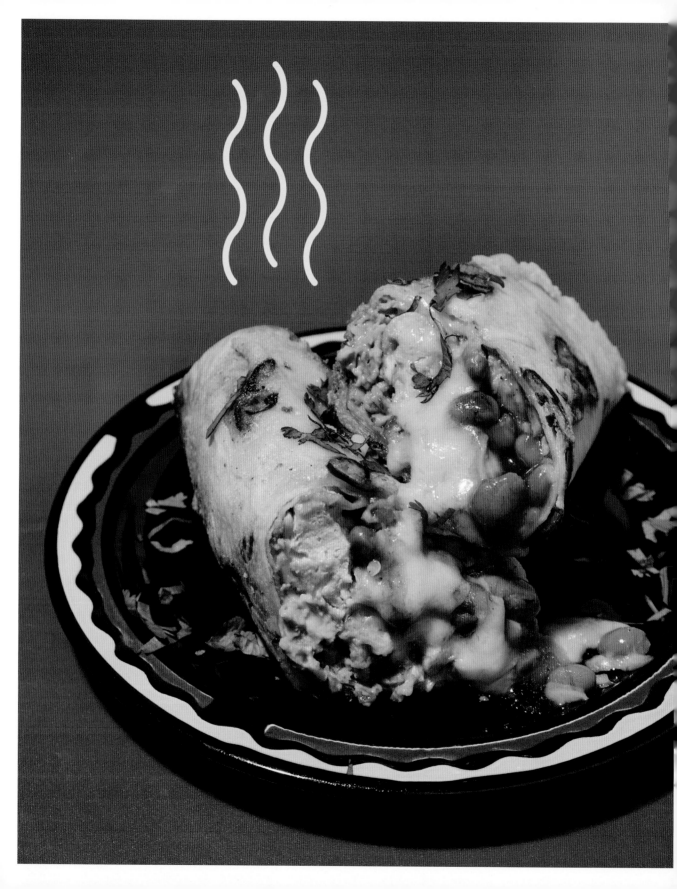

CHEESY CRUST BREAKFAST BURRITOS

PREP TIME: **10** MINUTES
COOK TIME: **15** MINUTES
DIFFICULTY: **MEDIUM**
SERVES: **2**
VEGGIE

Dropping Tex-Mex flavour bombs all over your brekkie. Roll this bad boy tortilla in a spicy cheese crust and douse in hot sauce, if you dare...

INGREDIENTS

200 g (7 oz) canned barbecue–flavoured baked beans, or regular baked beans

1 ripe avocado

juice of ½ lime

1 teaspoon salted butter

3 eggs, lightly beaten

2 flour tortillas

240 g (8½ oz) grated Cheddar cheese

2 green chillies, deseeded and finely sliced

coriander, roughly chopped

salt and pepper

hot sauce, to serve, (optional)

METHOD

1. Heat the baked beans in a saucepan over a low–medium heat for 4–5 minutes, or in a microwave for 2½ minutes on high.

2. Meanwhile, lightly mash the avocado in a small bowl, then squeeze over the lime juice and season with salt. Stir to combine and set aside.

3. Melt the butter in a large frying pan over a low heat and pour in the eggs. Once the eggs start to cook on the bottom, use a spatula to gently stir and fold the mixture. When the majority of the egg mixture is cooked, with a loose consistency, stir through some salt and pepper, then remove from the heat and set aside. The eggs will carry on cooking a little, off the heat.

4. Transfer the eggs to a plate, clean the frying pan and return to a medium heat. Gently warm the tortillas in the pan for 1 minute to soften, then remove and place on a board.

5. Spread the avocado across the bottom half of the tortillas and top each one with scrambled egg, baked beans and 40 g (1½ oz) of the cheese. Tightly roll the tortillas into burritos, starting from the base and folding in the sides as you roll to seal the edges.

6. Return the frying pan to a low–medium heat. Add half the sliced green chillies to the middle of the pan and scatter over half the remaining cheese. Once the cheese is melted and starting to turn golden, place a burrito in the pan and carefully roll it up in the cheese crust. Repeat this step with the remaining green chillies, cheese and burrito.

7. Slice the burritos in half to reveal their layered fillings, then scatter with coriander and serve with hot sauce, if you like.

PREP TIME: **5 MINUTES**

COOK TIME: **10 MINUTES**

DIFFICULTY: **EASY**

SERVES: **4**

MEAT

BACON EGG CUPS

Bin your egg cups for these CRISPY BACON egg cups. Make sure you've got your buttery toast soldiers for dunking in that ooooozy egg goodness.

INGREDIENTS

8 streaky bacon rashers

4 eggs

salt and pepper

4 slices of buttered toast, sliced into soldiers for dipping, to serve (optional)

METHOD

1. Preheat the grill to high.

2. Wrap 4 of the bacon rashers around the inside edges of 4 muffin moulds and cut the other 4 rashers in half so that you have 8 shorter rashers of bacon. Criss-cross these over the bases of the muffin moulds to form cups.

3. Grill the cups for 5 minutes, or until the bacon is cooked through but not crisp.

4. Crack an egg into each bacon cup and return to the grill for 5 minutes, or until the egg has set.

5. Season with salt and pepper and enjoy with toasted soldiers for dipping, if you like.

CHEESY CRUMPET LOAF

PREP TIME: **10 MINUTES**

COOK TIME: **30 MINUTES**

DIFFICULTY: **EASY**

SERVES: **4**

VEGAN

Crumpets don't need to just be crumpets. Elevate the ting, chuck in some vegan cheese and bake it so you can tear and share with the mandem.

INGREDIENTS

80 g (2¾ oz) vegan non–dairy spread, softened

4 teaspoons yeast extract spread, such as Marmite

8 crumpets

200 g (7 oz) grated vegan Cheddar–style cheese

METHOD

1. Preheat the oven to 180°C (350°F), Gas Mark 4 and line a loaf tin with nonstick baking paper.

2. Whisk the softened non–dairy spread with the yeast extract spread in a small bowl until fully combined.

3. Top the crumpets with this mixture, then divide 40 g (1½ oz) of the vegan cheese between them. Pile all the crumpets on top of each other and carefully transfer to the prepared loaf tin.

4. Sprinkle over the remaining vegan cheese and bake for 30 minutes until golden and bubbling.

5. Allow to cool for a few minutes before serving.

GLAZED DOUGHNUT BREAKFAST SANDOS

PREP TIME: **5 MINUTES**

COOK TIME: **15 MINUTES**

DIFFICULTY: **EASY**

SERVES: **2**

MEAT

Listen, don't you dare @ us until you actually try this. If using doughnuts for buns is wrong, then lock me up and throw away the key.

INGREDIENTS

4 smoked streaky bacon rashers

2 small burger patties

2 eggs

2 burger cheese slices

2 glazed doughnuts

METHOD

1. Preheat the grill to high and lay the bacon rashers and burger patties across a large foil-lined oven tray. Grill for 5 minutes on each side until cooked through and starting to crisp up.

2. Remove the tray from the grill and crack in the eggs alongside the burgers and bacon. Return to the grill and cook for 3-4 minutes, or until the eggs are cooked through. In the final minute, top the burgers with the cheese slices and allow to melt.

3. When ready to serve, slice the doughnuts in half horizontally and load them up with the cheesy burger patties, crispy bacon rashers and perfect grilled eggs. Serve immediately.

MAGIC SHELL BREAKFAST BOWLS

If breakfast's the most important meal of the day, you better make it a GOOD one. Whip up this magic brekkie bowl and smash the chocolate shell for a smoothie surprise!

INGREDIENTS

3 tablespoons coconut oil

200 g (7 oz) frozen summer berries

200 g (7 oz) vegan yogurt

75 ml (2½ fl oz) coconut milk (or any plant-based milk)

2 tablespoons hazelnut chocolate spread, such as Nutella

2 teaspoons chopped hazelnuts (optional)

2 tablespoons fresh raspberries (optional)

METHOD

1. Melt the coconut oil in a small saucepan over a low heat and set aside to cool a little.

2. Put the frozen berries, yogurt and coconut milk in a food processor or high-powered blender and blitz until smooth and thick. Cover and set aside in the refrigerator.

3. Stir the hazelnut chocolate spread through the melted coconut oil until fully combined.

4. Divide the thick smoothie mixture between 2 cereal bowls and pour over the melted chocolate mix. This should almost instantly set to a hard shell.

5. Top with chopped hazelnuts and raspberries, if you like, and dig in!

TIP:

Try swapping chocolate spread for speculoos spread and thank us later.

HONEY-NUT FRENCH TOAST

PREP TIME: **10 MINUTES**
COOK TIME: **10 MINUTES**
DIFFICULTY: **EASY**
SERVES: **2**
VEGGIE

I see your French toast and I raise you HONEY-NUT French toast. Eggy cinnamon-soaked brioche with a cheeky honey-nut crunch coat. Yes.

INGREDIENTS

50 g (1¾ oz) honey–nut flake cereal

2 eggs, lightly beaten

125 ml (4 fl oz) milk

½ teaspoon ground cinnamon

4 brioche slices

2 tablespoons salted butter

2 tablespoons maple syrup, to serve (optional)

METHOD

1. Measure the cereal into a bowl and lightly crush with a rolling pin.

2. Combine the eggs, milk and cinnamon in a separate wide, shallow bowl.

3. Dip the slices of brioche into the egg mixture and turn to coat, then coat in the crushed cereal.

4. Melt the butter in a large frying pan over a medium heat and gently fry the brioche slices for 3–5 minutes on each side until golden and crisp.

5. Serve with maple syrup.

CAUGHT LUNCHIN'

FOOD-WASTE HACKS

Don't be a WASTEMAN; save your leftover tings and whip them up into something beautiful.

BREADCRUMBS

Put stale or leftover bread, crusts and all, in a food processor and pulse to a crumb. These can be stored in the freezer for up to 3 months and can be used to coat chicken, fish and veg, or to thicken sauces. To use as a coating, defrost the crumbs, then spread them on a baking tray and toast in the oven at 180°C (350°F), Gas Mark 4, for 6–8 minutes until golden.

CHEESE RIND 'STOCK CUBE'

You know you a bougie chefileeni when you find a Parmesan rind at the back of the refrigerator. Or maybe you're a basic-b chef with a stale block of Cheddar back there: you know, the one that escaped the cling? Whatever it is, we got you. Just throw this in with your tomato sauce ingredients (see page 15) to add FLAVOURS and all-important sodium. You won't regret it.

HERBS FOR DAYZ

Found some rogue herbs chilling at the back of the refrigerator? Chop and freeze them (an ice-cube tray makes a great container), then add them to sauces as and when. Alternatively add the herbs, stalks 'n' all, to your bottle of olive oil for a chefileeni infusion!

CHILLI CHEESE CROUTONS

PREP TIME: **5 MINUTES**

COOK TIME: **6–8 MINUTES**

DIFFICULTY: **EASY**

SERVES: **4 as a snack or salad or soup topping**

VEGGIE

INGREDIENTS

4 slices of leftover or stale bread

3 tablespoons olive oil

1 teaspoon paprika

1 teaspoon sea salt flakes

2 tablespoons finely grated Cheddar cheese

METHOD

1. Preheat the oven to 180°C (350°F), Gas Mark 4. Line a baking tray with nonstick baking paper.

2. Slice the bread into bite–sized chunks and put them in a medium–sized bowl with the olive oil, paprika and salt. Toss everything together until the bread is well coated.

3. Spread the croutons across the prepared tray and sprinkle over the Cheddar.

4. Bake for 6-8 minutes until golden, crisp and melted. Perfect added to a salad, or just as a snack. Enjoy!

CINNAMON SHUGZ FRENCH TOAST BITES

PREP TIME: **5 MINUTES**

COOK TIME: **4 MINUTES**

DIFFICULTY: **EASY**

SERVES: **4 as a snack**

VEGGIE

INGREDIENTS

4 slices of leftover or stale bread

1 egg

2 tablespoons whole milk

½ teaspoon vanilla extract

2 teaspoons caster sugar

½ teaspoon ground cinnamon

1 tablespoon unsalted butter

METHOD

1. Stack up the slices of bread and slice them into squares or cubes.

2. Whisk the egg, milk and vanilla together in a medium bowl.

3. Combine the sugar and cinnamon in a separate shallow bowl.

4. Dip the bread slices in the egg mixture, ensuring they are well coated. Allow any excess egg mixture to drip off, then turn the bread in the cinnamon sugar.

5. Melt the butter in a frying pan and fry the bites for 2 minutes on each side until golden and lightly toasted. Enjoy as they are, or dipped in melted chocolate.

JUICE CUBES

Got a load of half lemons and/or limes knocking around the refrigerator? Squeeze the juice into an ice-cube tray, freeze and save for future cocktails and salad dressings!

BANANA PEEL PURÉE

Got spare banaynays chilling in the fruit bowl? Next time you make banana bread, try this madness: Save the peels (trust), put them in a saucepan and cover with water. Bring to a gentle simmer and simmer for 20 minutes. Drain and rinse the peels under cold running water to cool them down, then blitz them to a smooth purée in a food processor. Add the purée to your banana bread batter for a denser and all-round banging loaf!

Don't be a WASTEMAN

CANDIED PEEL

PREP TIME: **10 MINUTES**

COOK TIME: **30 MINUTES**

DIFFICULTY: **EASY**

MAKES: **A SMALL BOWL**

VEGAN

INGREDIENTS

2 unwaxed lemons or limes

400 ml (14 fl oz) water

130 g (4¾ oz) caster sugar

METHOD

1. Use a peeler to remove the zest from the lemons, then finely slice the zest into strips with a sharp knife.

2. Put the lemon zest in a small saucepan, then add the measured water and 100 g (3½ oz) of the caster sugar and bring to a gentle simmer. Simmer for 30 minutes, then drain through a sieve.

3. Pat the peel dry with kitchen paper and toss in the remaining sugar. Store in an airtight container for up to 2 weeks and use to garnish cakes and cocktails.

APPLE PEEL VODKA SOUR

PREP TIME: **5 MINUTES + 3–5 DAYS INFUSING**

COOK TIME: **NONE**

DIFFICULTY: **EASY**

MAKES: **70cl (1¼-pint) BOTTLE**

VEGAN

INGREDIENTS

6 apples, peel only (we recommend Granny Smith or cooking apples)

juice of ½ lemon

50 g (1¾ oz) granulated sugar

70 cl (1¼–pint) bottle of vodka

METHOD

1. Put the apple peel, lemon juice and sugar in a large airtight storage jar and top with the vodka. Seal the jar and store in the refrigerator for 3–5 days to infuse.

2. Strain the vodka into a bottle. Store in a cool, dry place. Enjoy on its own or with a mixer of your choice for a totally boujee apple cocktail.

PESTO BAKED EGGS

PREP TIME: **5 MINUTES**

COOK TIME: **12 MINUTES**

DIFFICULTY: **EASY**

SERVES: **2**

VEGGIE

For when you want something EASY and delicious. Lazy days and that. Dunk a hunk of bread in these sensational pesto baked eggs and RELAX.

INGREDIENTS

50 g (1¾ oz) grated mozzarella cheese

2 tablespoons vegetarian green pesto

2 eggs

½ teaspoon chilli flakes

2 thick sourdough bread slices

2 tablespoons olive oil

salt and pepper

METHOD

1. Preheat the oven to 180°C (350°F), Gas Mark 4.

2. Divide the grated mozzarella between 2 ovenproof ramekins and top with the green pesto, then crack an egg into each. Season with salt, pepper and the chilli flakes and bake in the oven for 12 minutes, or until the egg is cooked with a runny yolk.

3. Meanwhile, brush the sourdough with olive oil and toast in a frying pan for 2 minutes on each side over a medium–high heat. Season the toasted sourdough and slice into soldiers.

4. Serve the baked pesto eggs, hot out of the oven, with the sourdough soldiers for dipping.

ONE-PAN BLT PASTA SALAD

PREP TIME: **10 MINUTES**

COOK TIME: **15 MINUTES**

DIFFICULTY: **EASY**

SERVES: **4**

MEAT

When bacon, lettuce and tomato pair up with creamy, cheesy pasta, you better know you're in for a treat!

INGREDIENTS

160 g (5¾ oz) bacon lardons

400 ml (14 fl oz) whole milk

150 g (5½ oz) farfalle pasta

25 g (1 oz) finely grated Parmesan cheese

150 ml (¼ pint) double cream

200 g (7 oz) cherry tomatoes, halved

1 head of Cos lettuce, sliced

1 tablespoon chopped parsley leaves

pinch of cayenne pepper

salt and pepper

METHOD

1. Fry the bacon lardons in a large, deep frying pan with a well-fitting lid over a medium-high heat until crisp. Remove the lardons from the pan and set aside on a piece of kitchen paper to drain the excess fat.

2. Add the milk and pasta to the same pan and season with salt and pepper. Bring to the boil over a medium-high heat. Reduce the heat, cover and simmer for 10 minutes, until the pasta is cooked al dente and the liquid has thickened and been mostly absorbed. Remove the pan from the heat.

3. Stir through the Parmesan and double cream until the pasta is well coated. Add the drained bacon lardons, cherry tomatoes, lettuce and parsley and stir through until evenly combined.

4. Divide between 4 warmed bowls and season each with a pinch of cayenne pepper.

BLOODY MARY PRAWN COCKTAIL CUPS

The classic prawn cocktail with a shot of vodka to put hairs on your chest. Who needs a bowl when nature gave us leaves?

INGREDIENTS

100 g (3½ oz) mayonnaise

1 tablespoon tomato ketchup

2 teaspoons Tabasco sauce

½ teaspoon Worcestershire sauce

1 tablespoon vodka

juice of ½ lemon

¼ teaspoon salt

300 g (10½ oz) cooked king prawns

12 large leaves of Baby Gem lettuce

pinch of cayenne pepper

dill sprigs and lemon slices, to serve (optional)

METHOD

1. In a large bowl, combine the mayonnaise, ketchup, Tabasco, Worcestershire sauce, vodka, lemon juice and salt. Add the king prawns and stir, ensuring they are evenly coated.

2. Spoon the prawn mixture into the lettuce leaves and top with cayenne pepper, then serve with dill and lemon slices, if you like.

IN DA CLUB SANDWICH

PREP TIME: **15 MINUTES**
COOK TIME: **12 MINUTES**
DIFFICULTY: **EASY**
SERVES: **2**
VEGGIE

The Caught club sando is a STAPLE in the Caught Snackin' gang.

INGREDIENTS

6 white bread slices

9 tablespoons mayonnaise

1 tablespoon mustard (Dijon, American or wholegrain)

¼ head of lettuce

2 large tomatoes, sliced

4 Cheddar cheese slices

1 large avocado, sliced

25 g (1 oz) salt and vinegar or ready-salted crisps, plus more to serve (optional)

2 hard-boiled eggs, peeled and sliced

salt and pepper

METHOD

1. Spread both sides of each slice of bread with mayonnaise, using 1 tablespoon for each slice, and lightly toast in a frying or griddle pan for 2 minutes on each side.

2. Combine the remaining 3 tablespoons of mayonnaise with the mustard in a small bowl.

3. Now construct the club sandwiches, seasoning with salt and pepper as you build. Top 2 slices of toasted bread with the mustard mayonnaise, lettuce, sliced tomatoes and Cheddar cheese slices.

4. Now top each one with another slice of toasted bread, followed by the sliced avocado, a small handful of crisps and a sliced egg.

5. Top with the final slices of toasted bread and cut the sandwiches into quarters on the diagonal.

6. Skewer cocktail sticks through the sandwich quarters to hold them in place and serve with extra crisps on the side, if you like.

QUICK CAULIFLOWER MAC & CHEESE

PREP TIME: **10 MINUTES +
COOLING**

COOK TIME: **30 MINUTES**

DIFFICULTY: **EASY**

SERVES: **2**

VEGAN

The scrumptious lovechild of cauliflower cheese and macaroni cheese, topped with a crispy crumb top. PS, it's VEGAN.

INGREDIENTS

400 ml (14 fl oz) full-fat oat milk

½ cauliflower, cut into small florets

1 bay leaf

150 g (5½ oz) macaroni

1 tablespoon olive oil

200 g (7 oz) grated Cheddar-style vegan cheese

½ tablespoon American mustard or Dijon mustard

2 handfuls of cheese-flavoured tortilla chips, crushed to a fine crumb

salt and pepper

METHOD

1. Pour the oat milk into a large, deep frying pan with a well-fitting lid. Bring to a simmer over a medium heat. Add the cauliflower florets and bay leaf and season with salt and pepper. Cover and allow to poach for 20 minutes, until the cauliflower is cooked through.

2. Meanwhile, bring a pan of salted water to the boil and cook the macaroni for 8 minutes. Drain and stir through the olive oil to stop the pasta from sticking together.

3. Remove the cauliflower pan from the heat and allow to cool. Discard the bay leaf, then blend the cauliflower mixture in a food processor, or use a stick blender, until you have a thickened, creamy sauce.

4. Return the sauce to the pan and gently heat. Add the grated vegan cheese and mustard and stir until the cheese has melted. Tip in the cooked pasta and stir through, ensuring it is well coated in the sauce.

5. Preheat the grill to medium-high and transfer the contents of the pan into an ovenproof dish.

6. Top with the crumbled tortilla chips and place under the grill for 8-10 minutes, until golden on top. Dig in.

PREP TIME: **10 MINUTES**

COOK TIME: **18 MINUTES**

DIFFICULTY: **EASY**

SERVES: **2**

MEAT

CHEESEBURGER CRUNCH WRAP

Juicy cheeseburger fillings wrapped snug in a fluffy tortilla, with a secret ingredient to bring that CRUNCH.

INGREDIENTS

2 burger patties

4 streaky bacon rashers

2 burger cheese slices

2 large flour tortillas

2 tablespoons burger sauce (see page 185)

4 Iceberg lettuce leaves, sliced

½ large tomato, sliced

2 large gherkins, sliced

12 plain or cheese-flavoured tortilla chips

2 small flour tortillas

METHOD

1. Fry the burger patties and bacon rashers in a large frying pan, set over a medium-high heat, for 5-6 minutes on each side until golden-brown and cooked through. Remove from the heat and top the hot burgers with the cheese slices.

2. Spread the large tortillas with the burger sauce and construct the crunch wraps, starting with sliced Iceberg lettuce, sliced tomato and the cooked cheese burgers. Add the crispy bacon and sliced gherkins, then top each crunch wrap with 6 tortilla chips arranged in a circle, like a wheel.

3. Place a small tortilla over the top of each one, then fold the larger, base tortillas up and over the smaller ones to seal the crunch wraps.

4. Fry the crunch wraps in the same large frying pan (one at a time) over a medium-high heat for 2-3 minutes on each side until golden brown.

5. Halve the wraps to reveal their layers and tuck in.

ONE-TRAY TOMATO SOUP

PREP TIME: **10 MINUTES + COOLING**

COOK TIME: **40 MINUTES**

DIFFICULTY: **EASY**

SERVES: **4**

VEGGIE

Good soup. (If you know, you know.)

INGREDIENTS

1.4 kg (3 lb 2 oz) cherry tomatoes

2 red chillies

2 garlic bulbs, halved horizontally

2 red onions, halved

2–3 thyme sprigs

2 bunches of basil, plus baby leaves to serve (optional)

2 tablespoons olive oil

300 ml (½ pint) vegetable stock, at room temperature

100 g (3½ oz) crème fraîche

salt and pepper

crusty bread, to serve (optional)

METHOD

1. Preheat the oven to 180°C (350°F), Gas Mark 4.

2. Put the tomatoes, chillies, garlic and onions in a large roasting tray and top with the thyme, basil, olive oil and a generous pinch of salt and pepper.

3. Transfer to the oven and roast for 40 minutes, or until the tomato skins have become wrinkled and slightly charred. Remove from the oven and allow the vegetables to cool to room temperature, then squeeze the garlic cloves from their skins and discard the skins, along with the thyme sprigs.

4. Put the cooled vegetables into a food processor, along with the stock and crème fraîche, and blitz until smooth. Alternatively, use a bowl and a stick blender.

5. Pour the soup into a deep saucepan over a medium heat and warm through.

6. Season to taste and divide between 4 warmed bowls, topped with baby basil leaves and a thick slice of crusty bread, if you like.

PIZZA TOASTIE

This pizza toastie is oozing with cheese and tomato sauce. Feel free to do a little freestyle and play around with the fillings and that... Experimentation, you get me?

INGREDIENTS

4 white bread slices

25 g (1 oz) salted butter

8 tablespoons tomato pizza sauce (or see page 15)

250 g (9 oz) grated mozzarella cheese

1 large tomato, sliced

4 tablespoons finely grated vegetarian Parmesan cheese

small handful of basil leaves

salt and pepper

METHOD

1. Spread the slices of bread with the butter. Flip over 2 of the slices and spread with half the pizza sauce, then top with half the mozzarella cheese. Add the sliced tomato and season with salt and pepper, then scatter over 2 tablespoons of the Parmesan and half of the basil.

2. Top with the remaining slices of bread, buttered-sides up, and fry in an ovenproof pan over a medium-high heat for 2 minutes.

3. Meanwhile, preheat the grill to high.

4. Flip the toasties and spoon over the remaining pizza sauce, mozzarella and Parmesan and sprinkle on the rest of the basil.

5. Transfer the frying pan to the grill for 5 minutes, until the toasties are golden and bubbling.

6. Allow to cool slightly before serving.

Oozing with cheese and tomato sauce

KIM-CHEESE SPRING ROLLS

PREP TIME: **25 MINUTES**
COOK TIME: **10 MINUTES**
DIFFICULTY: **MEDIUM**
SERVES: **4 (MAKES 8)**
VEGAN

The combo of kimchi and cheese in these DIY spring rolls BANGS! Eat hot and crispy straight from the pan with a spicy sriracha drizzle.

INGREDIENTS

1 packet of vegetable–flavour instant noodles plus it's seasoning sachet

100 g (3½ oz) grated vegan cheese

16 rice paper sheets

50 g (1¾ oz) spinach leaves

300 g (10½ oz) kimchi

1 litre (1¾ pints) vegetable oil, for deep–frying

sriracha, to serve

METHOD

1. Cook the instant noodles according to the packet instructions. Stir half the vegan cheese through the noodles while they're still hot.

2. Construct the spring rolls, one by one. Dip a sheet of rice paper in room–temperature water and lay on a clean surface. Lay a handful of spinach leaves horizontally across the centre of the sheet and top with a spoonful of kimchi, then add an eighth of the cooked noodles and top with a generous sprinkling of cheese.

3. Lift the edge of the rice paper nearest to you over the filling and roll up tightly, tucking in the sides as you go to seal. Once rolled, wet another rice paper sheet and double–wrap the spring roll. Place on a wire rack while you construct the remaining spring rolls.

4. Heat the oil, in a deep saucepan with a well–fitting lid, to 180°C (350°F) and deep–fry the spring rolls, in 2 batches, for 2–3 minutes or until crispy and lightly golden. (See page 17 for deep–frying hacks.)

5. Place them on a sheet of kitchen paper to drain off any excess oil.

6. Serve immediately with a bowl of sriracha sauce for dipping.

TIP:
We double-wrap these bois to keep the filling intact while increasing all-important crunch levels.

PREP TIME: **30 MINUTES +
CHILLING**
COOK TIME: **15 MINUTES**
DIFFICULTY: **MEDIUM**
SERVES: **2–3**
FISH

ICE-CUBE TRAY SUSHI

People will be mind-blown at the shubz with this sushi ice-cube hack, trust me. Satisfying sushi bites topped with all ya favourite fishy flavours. Be sure to use rice vinegar here, as it's sweeter than regular vinegar.

INGREDIENTS

250 g (9 oz) sushi rice, or sticky rice

1 teaspoon white rice vinegar

2 tablespoons vegetable oil

100 g (3½ oz) smoked salmon

⅙ cucumber, peeled into ribbons and sliced into 5 cm (2–inch) lengths

6 cooked king prawns

1 avocado, halved, 1 half sliced, 1 half mashed

2 tablespoons sriracha mayonnaise

3 sheets of salted seaweed thins, cut into fine ribbons with scissors

soy sauce, to serve

A mind-blowing sushi ice-cube hack, trust me

METHOD

1. Weigh the rice into a bowl, cover with cold water, then stir and drain. Repeat this process 3 times to wash the rice.

2. Put the washed rice in a medium–sized saucepan with a well–fitting lid and pour over 300 ml (½ pint) cold water. Cover with the lid and bring to a gentle simmer over a low-medium heat. This should take about 10 minutes. Once simmering (you will hear it gently bubbling), avoid removing the lid. Reduce the heat to low for 5 minutes, then turn off the heat and set aside, lid on, for 15 minutes.

3. Transfer the cooked rice to a large baking sheet. Sprinkle over the vinegar and gently mix, then spread it out into a thin layer with a spatula. This will help the rice to cool quickly.

4. When the rice is cool, start making the sushi. Lightly oil your ice–cube tray/s. Add slices of smoked salmon to 6 of the ice-cube compartments, cucumber to the next 6, a prawn to each of the next 6 and sliced avocado to the final 6 compartments.

5. Spoon the sushi rice into each compartment and press it down with a spatula. Cover the tray/s and chill in the refrigerator for at least 20 minutes until the rice is firm.

6. When ready to serve, turn the sushi out on to a board or plate and top with spoonfuls of mashed avocado, sriracha mayo or shredded seaweed. Serve with soy sauce for dipping.

ONE-POT STICKY COLA WINGS

PREP TIME: **5 MINUTES**
COOK TIME: **45 MINUTES**
DIFFICULTY: **EASY**
SERVES: **4**
MEAT

These wings are gonna be a bit of a sticky sitch. Still, cola-infused for the win, and a sweet way to upgrade your basic wings.

INGREDIENTS

50 ml (2 fl oz) vegetable oil

1 kg (2 lb 4 oz) chicken wings

1 teaspoon salt

500 ml (18 fl oz) regular cola (not diet)

2 tablespoons soy sauce

2 star anise

1 tablespoon finely chopped garlic

2 spring onions, sliced

1 teaspoon white sesame seeds

250 g (9 oz) sticky rice or raw-slaw, to serve (optional)

METHOD

1. Heat the vegetable oil in a large, deep frying pan with a well-fitting lid over a medium-high heat.

2. Pat dry the chicken wings with kitchen paper and prick each one 4–5 times with a cocktail stick or skewer. Season with the salt and fry the wings, in batches, for 5 minutes on each side until golden and starting to crisp up.

3. Return all of the wings to the pan. Reduce the heat and pour in the cola and soy sauce, along with the star anise and garlic. Cover with the lid and simmer for 15 minutes.

4. Remove the lid and increase the heat to reduce the cola liquid to a sweet and sticky sauce. This should take about 10 minutes.

5. Once the sauce has reduced and coats the wings nicely, remove from the heat and serve on plates, topped with spring onions and sesame seeds. Serve with sticky rice or Asian-style slaw, if you like.

INSTANT NOODZ MAYO MAKEOVER

Everyone deserves a glow-up, no? Even instant noodz... give them a little contour and witness the flavours and vibes TAKE OFF!

INGREDIENTS

4 eggs

2 packets of vegetable–flavour instant noodles plus their seasoning sachets

2 garlic cloves, very finely chopped

2 tablespoons mayonnaise

1 teaspoon soy sauce

1 spring onion, sliced

1 teaspoon mixed sesame seeds

METHOD

1. Bring a saucepan of water to the boil. Add 2 of the eggs and cook for 7 minutes, then remove with a slotted spoon and put the eggs in a bowl of cold water. Do not tip away the boiling water. Once cool enough to handle, carefully peel the eggs and set aside.

2. Cook the noodles, without their seasoning sachets, in the reserved boiling water for 3 minutes. Reserve 2-3 tablespoons of the noodle water in a small bowl, then drain the noodles.

3. In a separate, large bowl, lightly beat the remaining eggs with the contents of the seasoning sachets, along with the garlic, mayonnaise and soy sauce. Add the reserved noodle water, 1 tablespoon at a time, and whisk through. Add the noodles and fold them through the sauce until evenly coated.

4. Divide the noodles between 2 warmed bowls and top with the soft–boiled eggs, sliced in half to reveal their soft yolks. Scatter over the spring onion and sesame seeds and serve.

FISH FINGER TACOS

PREP TIME: **15 MINUTES**

COOK TIME: **15 MINUTES**

DIFFICULTY: **EASY**

SERVES: **2**

FISH

Don't know what to do with the fish fingers in your freezer? Level them up and try these tasty, tangy tacos with a citrus mango salsa.

INGREDIENTS

8 frozen fish fingers

½ mango, peeled, pitted and chopped

¼ red onion, sliced

1–2 jalapeños, deseeded and sliced

1 teaspoon chopped coriander

juice of ½ lime

4 small flour tortillas

2 large avocados, mashed

1 Baby Gem lettuce, sliced

3 tbsp sriracha mayonnaise

salt and pepper

METHOD

1. Preheat the oven to 230°C (450°F), Gas Mark 8. Lay the frozen fish fingers out across an oven tray and cook for 12–15 minutes.

2. Meanwhile, in a medium bowl, combine the mango, red onion, jalapeño(s), coriander, lime juice and a pinch of salt and pepper to season.

3. Bend the tortillas in half to mimic a taco shell and slot into the toaster. Toast for 2 minutes or until they crisp up and hold their shape.

4. Spoon the mashed avocado into the base of the tacos and top with sliced lettuce, 2 fish fingers per taco and a generous spoonful of mango salsa. Drizzle over sriracha mayonnaise and enjoy.

TIP:
We beg you try these with scampi too.

CAULIFLOWER BASE PIZZA

PREP TIME: **10 MINUTES**
COOK TIME: **60 MINUTES**
DIFFICULTY: **EASY**
SERVES: **1–2**
VEGGIE

This no-dough pizza will have you shook when you try the crispy cauli base. Top with tomato sauce, melted cheese and colourful veggies and bosh that nosh.

INGREDIENTS

1 small cauliflower (approx. 750 g, 1lb 10 oz), cut into florets

4 tablespoons olive oil

25 g (1 oz) finely grated vegetarian Parmesan cheese

200 g (7 oz) grated mozzarella cheese

1 egg

75 ml (2½ fl oz / 5 tablespoons) tomato pizza sauce (or see page 15)

½ large tomato, sliced

¼ yellow pepper, sliced

45 g (1½ oz) chestnut mushrooms, sliced

salt and pepper

handful of basil leaves, to serve

METHOD

1. Preheat the oven to 160°C (325°F), Gas Mark 3. Blitz the cauliflower in a food processor, using the pulse setting, until you have a fine crumb.

2. Transfer the cauliflower to a large baking tray and spread it into a thin layer. Drizzle with 2 tablespoons of olive oil and season with salt and pepper. Bake for 12–15 minutes until cooked through and pale golden.

3. Remove the cooked cauliflower from the oven and increase the oven temperature to 180°C (350°F), Gas Mark 4.

4. When cool, pile the cooked cauliflower into a clean tea towel. Bring the corners of the towel over the top to seal and squeeze out any moisture over the sink.

5. In a large bowl, combine the cooked cauliflower with the Parmesan, half the mozzarella, the egg and 1 tablespoon of olive oil, and season with some salt and pepper. The mixture should come together into a thick dough.

6. Line the baking tray with nonstick baking paper. Transfer the cauliflower dough on to the baking tray, flattening and shaping it into a disc, roughly 1 cm (½ inch) thick.

7. Bake for 30 minutes, then top with the tomato sauce, the remaining mozzarella and the sliced vegetables. Drizzle with the remaining tablespoon of olive oil and season with salt and pepper. Bake for another 15 minutes. Serve, sliced and topped with basil leaves.

5-MINUTE CHILLI OIL NOODLES

Slurp these thick udon noodz coated in spicy chilli sauce and wait for your taste buds to take off! Made in five minutes, eaten in five seconds.

INGREDIENTS

150 g (5½ oz) thick udon noodles

1 tablespoon chilli flakes

1 garlic clove, very finely chopped

1 tablespoon sesame oil

1 tablespoon chilli oil

1 tablespoon mixed sesame seeds

1 tablespoon light soy sauce

3 tablespoons vegetable oil

salt and pepper

To serve (all optional)

steamed pak choi

1 spring onion, sliced

1 red chilli, finely chopped

METHOD

1. Cook the udon noodles according to the packet instructions.

2. In a medium–large bowl, combine the chilli flakes, garlic, sesame oil, chilli oil, sesame seeds and soy sauce.

3. Heat the vegetable oil in a small saucepan over a medium heat for 2 minutes, then pour this over the chilli mixture and stir to combine.

4. Add the cooked noodles and stir until they are well coated. Serve in a bowl with steamed pak choi, sprinkled with spring onion and red chilli, if you like.

Slurp these thick udon noodz

CHEESY HOT DOG ROLLS

PREP TIME: **20 MINUTES**
COOK TIME: **20 MINUTES**
DIFFICULTY: **EASY**
SERVES: **2–4**
MEAT

If you want more rolls, look no further. An American hot dog in sausage-roll camouflage, oozing with cheesy goodness and tangy mustard.

INGREDIENTS

320 g (11½ oz) sheet of shop–bought puff pastry

1 tablespoon plain flour, to dust

4 tablespoons American mustard

90 g (3¼ oz) grated Cheddar cheese

1 egg, lightly beaten

4 jumbo hot dogs

your favourite sauce, to serve

METHOD

1. Preheat the oven to 200°C (400°F), Gas Mark 6.

2. Put the pastry sheet on a lightly floured surface and gently roll it out so it is about 2.5 cm (1 inch) longer and wider than its original size. Slice the sheet of puff pastry in half lengthways, so you have 2 long rectangular sheets.

3. Leaving roughly 2 cm (¾ inch) along one of the long edges of each sheet bare, spread each pastry sheet with the mustard and top with the Cheddar. Brush the bare strip with the egg; this will act as a glue to seal the rolls.

4. Arrange the hot dogs (2 per sheet) lengthways over the cheese and roll them up in the pastry, sealing them along the egg–brushed edge. You will have 2 large sausage rolls.

5. Slice the sausage rolls into bite–sized pieces, roughly 5 cm (2 inches) wide, and arrange these on an oven tray. Brush with the remaining egg and bake in the oven for 20 minutes, until puffed out and golden.

6. Serve with your favourite dipping sauce.

CORONATION TUNA MELT JACKETS

PREP TIME: **10 MINUTES**
COOK TIME: **20 MINUTES**
DIFFICULTY: **EASY**
SERVES: **4**
FISH

Why be basic with your jacket when you can turn up the flavours with a coronation drop? I'm talking spices, that sweet chutney and melty cheese VIBES!

INGREDIENTS

4 baking potatoes

400 g (14 oz) canned line–caught tuna

80 g (2¾ oz) mayonnaise

5 teaspoons mild curry powder

1 teaspoon ground turmeric

8 teaspoons mango chutney

2 spring onions, sliced

50 g (1¾ oz) grated Red Leicester cheese

salt and pepper

To serve (all optional)

chopped coriander

Greek yogurt

METHOD

1. Preheat the oven to 220°C (425°F), Gas mark 7.

2. Using a sharp knife, prick each potato 4-5 times; this will allow any steam to escape as it cooks. Microwave on high for 10 minutes, turning after 5 minutes. Allow to cool.

3. Meanwhile, in a medium–large bowl, combine the tuna, mayonnaise, curry powder, turmeric, half the mango chutney and the spring onions. Season with salt and pepper.

4. With a sharp knife, carefully cut a large circle in the centre of each potato and hollow out the fluffy filling. Add this to the tuna mixture.

5. Generously spoon the curried tuna–and–potato mixture into the jackets and top with the grated cheese. Place on a baking tray and bake for 5-10 minutes until the cheese is melted and bubbling.

6. Serve the potatoes topped with the remaining mango chutney, along with some coriander and a dollop of yogurt, if you like.

SPEEDY LASAGNE POCKETS

PREP TIME: **15 MINUTES**
COOK TIME: **20 MINUTES**
DIFFICULTY: **EASY**
SERVES: **4–6**
MEAT

Who wants to waste their sweet time whipping up a long-ass lasagne when you can make a speedy and sexy lasagne pocket?

INGREDIENTS

12 fresh lasagne sheets

500 g (1 lb 2 oz) mozzarella slices

400 g (14 oz) shop–bought bechamel sauce

350 g (12 oz) shop–bought bolognese sauce

250 g (9 oz) grated mozzarella cheese

olive oil

salt and pepper

basil leaves

mixed leaf salad, to serve (optional)

METHOD

1. Preheat the oven to 180°C (350°F), Gas Mark 4 and line a baking tray with nonstick baking paper.

2. Lay the lasagne sheets across a deep oven tray. Boil the kettle and then pour over the boiled water. Allow the sheets to soak for 2 minutes until softened.

3. Carefully remove the lasagne sheets from the hot water and place on a chopping board, stacked up in a neat pile. Using a sharp knife, trim roughly 3 cm (1¼ inches) off the long edge of each sheet, to make them a little thinner. This will make the folding process easier and will result in neater pockets.

4. Lay a lasagne sheet, vertically, on a board or plate and place a slice of mozzarella in the centre. Top the mozzarella with a spoonful of creamy bechamel sauce.

5. Now add another lasagne sheet over the top, this time horizontally so it makes a cross shape with the first. Add another slice of mozzarella to the centre of the second sheet, followed by a spoonful of the bolognese.

6. Starting with the bottom lasagne sheet, fold the bare edges up and over the bolognese. Finish with another spoonful of creamy lasagne sauce and a generous sprinkling of grated mozzarella.

7. Place the pockets on the prepared baking tray, then drizzle with olive oil and season with salt and pepper. Bake for 20 minutes until golden and bubbling.

8. Top with basil leaves and serve, with a mixed leaf salad on the side, if you like.

CAUGHT PLAYLIST

Part of the prep is setting the vibes. Here are Spotify codes to 2 playlists we listen to while cooking. We will be updating them regularly.

Garage playlist

Vibes playlist

CAUGHT
DININ'

DARK 'N' STORMY RIBS

PREP TIME: **10 MINUTES**

COOK TIME: **40 MINUTES**

DIFFICULTY: **EASY**

SERVES: **2–4**

MEAT

There are two Rs in life that matter: rum and ribs, in that order. This recipe will have you sweet, sticky and sensational ribs in an hour – yes, really. Hold tight it's gonna get STORMY out there.

INGREDIENTS

1.2 kg (2 lb 11 oz) rack of pork ribs

2 tablespoons salt

1.5 litres (2¾ pints) ginger beer

180 g (6 oz) soft dark brown sugar

230 ml (8 fl oz) dark rum

2 tablespoons soy sauce

2 teaspoons cayenne pepper

2 teaspoons garlic powder

½ teaspoon chilli flakes

coleslaw and grilled sweetcorn cobettes, to serve (optional)

METHOD

1. Put the ribs in a large saucepan with 1 tablespoon of the salt and cover with 1 litre (1¾ pints) of the ginger beer. Bring to a gentle simmer over a medium heat. Simmer for 30 minutes, skimming the froth off the top with a large spoon after 10 minutes.

2. Meanwhile, make the glaze. Combine 150 g (5½ oz) of the sugar, with the remaining ginger beer, the dark rum and the soy sauce in a large frying pan. Bring to a gentle simmer over a low–medium heat. Simmer the sauce for 15 minutes, stirring occasionally, until it has reduced to a syrup–like consistency.

3. Remove from the heat and allow to cool for 10 minutes or so. The glaze will continue to thicken as it cools.

4. After 20 minutes, remove the ribs from the ginger beer, pouring this away.

5. Combine the remaining sugar and salt in a small bowl, along with the cayenne pepper, garlic powder and chilli flakes. Rub this over the ribs and lay them across a wire rack with a baking tray underneath.

6. Preheat the grill to high and place the ribs underneath for 10 minutes, turning and brushing them generously with the glaze halfway through. The ribs will be sticky and caramelised.

7. Portion up the ribs and serve with any remaining glaze poured over, alongside some coleslaw and grilled sweetcorn cobettes, if you like.

BANG BANG SHRIMP

If you're looking to flex on the mandem or impress the sweet ones, this will do it. Crunchy textures are on point, looking very chefileeni with this one...

INGREDIENTS

2 tablespoons mayonnaise

2 teaspoons sriracha

2 teaspoons sweet chilli sauce

80 g (2¾ oz) hot chilli–flavoured corn puffs

40 g (1½ oz) panko breadcrumbs

40 g (1½ oz) cornflour

2 eggs, lightly beaten

180 g (6 oz) large raw king prawns

250 ml (9 fl oz) vegetable oil, for deep–frying

250 g (9 oz) sticky rice (optional)

1 spring onion, sliced (optional)

METHOD

1. Combine the mayonnaise, sriracha and chilli sauce in a small bowl and set aside. This is your bang bang sauce.

2. Put the chilli–flavoured corn puffs in a medium–sized bowl and gently crush to a crumb using a rolling pin. Stir through the panko breadcrumbs until well combined. Put the cornflour in a second bowl and the beaten egg in a third.

3. Pat dry the prawns with kitchen paper, then coat in cornflour, followed by the beaten egg and finally the chilli–panko crumb. Set aside on a plate.

4. Heat the oil to 180°C (350°F) in a frying pan with a well–fitting lid over a medium heat and deep–fry the prawns, in 2 batches, for 4 minutes on each side until evenly golden and crisp. Remove from the pan and drain on kitchen paper. (See page 17 for deep–frying hacks.)

5. Serve the prawns with the bang bang sauce, on a bed of sticky rice and scattered with spring onion, if you like.

TIP:
Double the cornflour, egg and panko crumb mix and coat the prawns twice for extra-crispy shrimp.

CREAMY VODKA PASTA

PREP TIME: **15 MINUTES**
COOK TIME: **15 MINUTES**
DIFFICULTY: **EASY**
SERVES: **4**
VEGGIE

Believe me when I tell you this sauce is so silky that it glistens... Rich, creamy and a little bit naughty with the voddy.

INGREDIENTS

1 onion, finely chopped

2 garlic cloves, very finely chopped

2 red chillies, deseeded and finely chopped

250 ml (9 fl oz) double cream

250 ml (9 fl oz) tomato passata

500 g (1 lb 2 oz) spaghetti

900 ml (32 fl oz) water

60 g (2¼ oz) finely grated vegetarian Parmesan cheese

25 ml (1 fl oz) shot of vodka

handful of basil leaves

salt and pepper

METHOD

1. Put the onion, garlic, chillies, cream, passata, spaghetti and measured water into a large, deep frying pan with a well–fitting lid.

2. Cover and bring to the boil over a medium–high heat, then reduce the heat to low and simmer for 12 minutes, or until the pasta is cooked and has absorbed some of the sauce.

3. Add the Parmesan and vodka and stir through, cooking for a further 2–3 minutes.

4. Divide between 4 warmed bowls and serve, topped with a handful of basil leaves.

ONE-POT-WONDER BAKED TOMATO RISOTTO

PREP TIME: **5 MINUTES**

COOK TIME: **1 HOUR**

DIFFICULTY: **EASY**

SERVES: **4**

VEGGIE

This boi really be a one-pot-WONDER when it's this darn tasty! The creamy baked feta melted with that tangy tomato sauce... Unbelievable scenes.

INGREDIENTS

750 g (1 lb 10 oz) cherry tomatoes

200 g (7 oz) block of feta cheese

small bunch of basil

3 tablespoons olive oil, plus extra to serve

300 g (10½ oz) arborio rice

65 ml (2¼ fl oz) white wine

350 ml (12 fl oz) vegetable stock

salt and pepper

METHOD

1. Preheat the oven to 180°C (350°F), Gas Mark 4.

2. Tip the cherry tomatoes into an oven dish. Place the block of feta in the centre. Add the basil, then drizzle with the 3 tablespoons of olive oil and season generously with salt and pepper. Bake for 25 minutes until the tomatoes are starting to caramelise and the feta has softened and melted slightly.

3. Remove the dish from the oven, discard the basil and mix the feta and tomatoes together to make a rich, creamy sauce.

4. Stir in the rice, wine and stock and return to the oven for 30–35 minutes, until the rice is cooked through and has expanded, absorbing the stock. Serve in warmed bowls.

EASY PEKING FUN GUY PANCAKES

Be a fun guy with these shroom-packed Peking pancakes, finessed with a crunch from all them fresh veggies.

INGREDIENTS

For the hoisin sauce

1 tablespoon sesame oil

3 tablespoons soy sauce

2 tablespoons rice wine vinegar

1 tablespoon sriracha

1 tablespoon honey

For the pancakes

8 large portobello mushrooms

8 Chinese pancakes

½ cucumber, deseeded and sliced into matchsticks

2 spring onions, sliced into strips

2 teaspoons white sesame seeds

METHOD

1. Preheat the oven to 160°C (325°F), Gas Mark 3.

2. Put all the hoisin sauce ingredients into a small bowl and stir to combine.

3. Lay the mushrooms across a baking tray and pour over the sauce, then bake for 30 minutes until cooked through and golden.

4. Remove from the oven and shred the mushrooms with 2 forks, mixing them through the sauce as you do so.

5. Transfer the mushrooms to a serving dish and serve alongside the other ingredients for people to build their pancakes themselves.

6. To construct the pancakes, simply add a spoonful of the mushrooms to a pancake and top with cucumber, spring onion and a pinch of sesame seeds. Roll up and enjoy!

Be a fun guy with these shroom-packed pancakes

QUICK GNOCCHI WITH A GREEN CHEESE SAUCE

PREP TIME: **15 MINUTES**
COOK TIME: **15 MINUTES**
DIFFICULTY: **EASY**
SERVES: **2**
VEGGIE

Don't be shook! This easy DIY gnocchi will make you look like a top chefileeni. We won't tell anyone you used pre-made mash – we got you.

INGREDIENTS

190 g (6¾ oz) plain flour, plus more to dust

½ teaspoon salt

400 g (14 oz) shop–bought or leftover mashed potato

3 garlic cloves, very finely chopped

30 g (1 oz) finely grated vegetarian Parmesan cheese

1 egg, lightly beaten

35 g (1¼ oz) unsalted butter

30 g (1 oz) bunch of basil

250 ml (9 fl oz) whole milk

150 g (5½ oz) grated Cheddar cheese

30 g (1 oz) toasted breadcrumbs (see page 88)

pepper

METHOD

1. Bring a large pan of salted water to the boil.

2. Meanwhile, put 170 g (6 oz) of the flour in a bowl with the salt, mashed potato, garlic, Parmesan and egg. Combine to make a dough. Transfer the dough to a floured surface. Knead the dough for no more than 1 minute until soft but smooth and holding its shape. Dust in a little more flour if the dough is too loose and sticky.

3. Divide the dough into quarters, rolling each into a long sausage about 2.5 cm (1 inch) thick. Cut the sausages into 2.5 cm (1 inch) pieces and boil for 5–6 minutes, or until the gnocchi start to float. Drain.

4. Melt 15 g (½ oz) of the butter in a frying pan over a medium heat and fry the drained gnocchi in batches for 2–3 minutes on each side.

5. Meanwhile, in a blender, blend the basil and 50 ml (2 fl oz) of the milk until you have a vibrant green sauce.

6. Melt the remaining butter in a saucepan over a medium heat and whisk in the remaining 20 g (¾ oz) flour. Cook for 2 minutes, whisking, until pale golden. Pour in the remaining 200 ml (7 fl oz) milk, bit by bit, and whisk after each addition until you have a smooth sauce.

7. Cook the sauce for 2 minutes until thickened. Add the Cheddar, stirring, until rich and creamy. Stir through the basil mixture; this will turn the sauce a vibrant green. Taste and season with a little salt and pepper.

8. Serve the gnocchi with the green cheese sauce poured over and a generous sprinkle of toasted breadcrumbs.

10-MINUTE THAI GREEN CURRY

Fine Thai cuisine in 10 minutes? MADNESS. Blessed with health, thanks to all them veggies.

INGREDIENTS

1 tablespoon coconut oil

2 garlic cloves, sliced

2 green Thai chillies, sliced

½ aubergine, cut into small cubes

100 g (3½ oz) baby sweetcorn

100 g (3½ oz) sugar snap peas

1 red pepper, sliced

400 ml (14 fl oz) can of coconut milk

2 tablespoons vegan Thai green curry paste

250 g (9 oz) cooked Thai jasmine microwaveable rice pouch

salt and pepper

small handful of Thai basil leaves, or coriander, to serve (optional)

METHOD

1. Melt the coconut oil in a large, deep frying pan, over a medium-high heat. Add the garlic, chillies, aubergine, baby sweetcorn, sugar snap peas and red pepper. Fry for 2 minutes, stirring, until the vegetables have started to soften and brown a little.

2. Pour over the coconut milk and bring to the boil, then reduce the heat to a simmer.

3. Stir in the Thai green curry paste and simmer for 8 minutes.

4. Meanwhile, microwave the rice according to the packet instructions.

5. Taste the curry and season with salt and pepper accordingly, then remove from the heat and stir through the Thai basil or coriander, if using. Divide the jasmine rice and curry between warmed bowls and serve.

RUSTIC RAVIOLI LASAGNE

PREP TIME: **10 MINUTES**
COOK TIME: **25 MINUTES**
DIFFICULTY: **EASY**
SERVES: **4**
VEGGIE

This hot twist on lasagne is a banger! Why use basic-b pasta sheets when you can save time and increase flavours with ravioli layers?

INGREDIENTS

450 ml (16 fl oz) tomato pizza sauce (or see page 15)

500 g (1 lb 2 oz) fresh vegetarian ravioli (such as butternut squash or mushroom filling)

18 mozzarella cheese slices

drizzle of olive oil

salt and pepper

METHOD

1. Preheat the oven to 190°C (375°F), Gas Mark 5.

2. Pour one–third of the tomato sauce across the base of a large oven dish and top with one–third of the ravioli, in a single layer. Arrange 6 slices of mozzarella across the top and season with salt and pepper. Repeat this layering twice more.

3. Drizzle with olive oil and bake for 25 minutes, until golden and bubbling, then serve.

Save time and increase flavours with ravioli

VEGGIE TIKKA MASALA NAAN BOWLS

Make yourself a fresh naan bowl filled with veggie masala curry. Save the washing-up and feed your soul!

INGREDIENTS

For the naan bowls

200 g (7 oz) self-raising flour

140 g (5 oz) Greek-style vegan yogurt

2 tablespoons olive oil, for brushing and drizzling

salt and pepper

For the tikka masala

2 tablespoons vegetable oil

½ onion, finely chopped

2 garlic cloves, very finely chopped

1 teaspoon peeled and finely grated fresh root ginger

2 red chillies, deseeded and sliced

1 teaspoon garam masala

½ teaspoon ground turmeric

2 sweet potatoes, peeled and cubed

1 green pepper, sliced

180 g (6 oz) canned chickpeas (drained weight)

350 ml (12 fl oz) canned coconut milk

2 tablespoons tomato purée

250 g (9 oz) cooked basmati rice and chopped coriander, to serve (optional)

METHOD

1. Preheat the oven to 190°C (375°F), Gas Mark 5.

2. Combine the self-raising flour and vegan yogurt in a mixing bowl, along with some salt and pepper, until you have a smooth dough. Wrap in clingfilm and set aside to rest.

3. Meanwhile, heat the vegetable oil in a large, deep frying pan over a medium heat. Sweat the onion, garlic, ginger and chillies with the garam masala and turmeric.

4. After about 10 minutes, add the sweet potatoes, green pepper and chickpeas, and cook for a further 5 minutes, stirring.

5. Pour in the coconut milk and tomato purée and stir through, then reduce the heat and simmer for 20 minutes.

6. Meanwhile, divide the rested dough into 4 balls and flatten each ball into a disc roughly ½ cm (¼ inch) thick. Brush 4 ovenproof bowls with olive oil and place a disc of dough inside each bowl. The bowls will act as a mould for the naans, shaping them as they bake.

7. Drizzle the dough with the remaining olive oil, season with salt and pepper and bake for 25-30 minutes until golden.

8. Remove the bowls from the oven and carefully turn out the naans. Spoon the tikka masala into the naan bowls. Top with coriander and serve with basmati rice, if you like.

50-GARLIC CHICKEN KIEVS

PREP TIME: **15 MINUTES + COOLING + CHILLING**

COOK TIME: **65 MINUTES**

DIFFICULTY: **MEDIUM**

SERVES: **4**

MEAT

What's the most garlic you've ever seen in a recipe? Don't answer that, because we topped everyone with 50 cloves. YES, 50!

INGREDIENTS

5 small garlic bulbs

60 ml (4 tablespoons) olive oil

250 g (9 oz) breadcrumbs (see page 88)

200 g (7 oz) salted butter, at room temperature

30 g (1 oz) chopped parsley leaves

100 g (3½ oz) finely grated Parmesan cheese, or any other hard cheese

½ teaspoon chilli flakes

4 large chicken breasts

50 g (1¾ oz) plain flour

2 eggs, lightly beaten

salt and pepper

chips or mash and steamed greens, to serve (optional)

METHOD

1. Preheat the oven to 180°C (350°F), Gas Mark 4.

2. Slice the tops off the garlic bulbs and discard. Lay the bulbs across a sheet of foil, drizzle with the olive oil and season with salt and pepper. Bake for 35 minutes, until soft, golden and fragrant.

3. Meanwhile, tip the breadcrumbs onto a baking tray and toast in the oven for 8-10 minutes, or until pale golden. Set aside to cool. If toasting in advance, allow to cool and store in an airtight container.

4. When the garlic is out of the oven and has cooled enough to handle, squeeze the soft cloves from their skins into a medium-sized bowl (you should have about 50 cloves). Add the soft butter, chopped parsley, Parmesan and chilli flakes, and season with salt and pepper. Stir or whisk until well combined and transfer to a piece of clingfilm or nonstick baking paper. Shape the flavoured butter into a chunky cylinder and chill in the refrigerator for 20 minutes.

5. When the butter has hardened, slice it into 4 discs roughly 2 cm (¾ inch) thick. Using a sharp knife, slice into the chicken breasts along one side to create a pocket. Push a disc of garlic butter into each breast and press the pocket closed.

6. Put the flour, eggs and - into 3 separate bowls.

7. Coat the chicken breasts in flour, then in egg and finally in breadcrumbs. Repeat the egg and breadcrumb steps to double-seal the chicken breasts. This will help to stop the garlic butter from spilling out during baking and ensure your Kievs are extra crispy!

8. Lay the Kievs on a wire rack set over a baking tray and bake for 25-30 minutes, or until cooked through. Serve with chips or mash and steamed greens, if you like.

Watch the pink POP in our magical rice bowl

UNICORN RICE BOWLS

PREP TIME: **10 MINUTES**
COOK TIME: **30 MINUTES**
DIFFICULTY: **EASY**
SERVES: **2**
VEGAN

Colours on colours! Squeeze lime over this rice and watch the pink POP in our magical rice bowl. Yes, with vegan cheese puffs... AND WHAT?

INGREDIENTS

150 ml (¼ pint) white wine vinegar

1 tablespoon caster sugar

1 large carrot, peeled into ribbons

½ cucumber, peeled into ribbons

¼ red cabbage, finely sliced

150 g (5½ oz) Thai sticky rice

juice of 1 lime

1 avocado, sliced

small handful of vegan cheese puffs

1 tablespoon vegan mayonnaise

2 tablespoons sriracha

2 tablespoons coriander leaves, torn

½ teaspoon mixed sesame seeds

TIP:
Swap the rice for 200 g (7 oz) vermicelli noodles to make mermaid hair bowls.

METHOD

1. Combine the white wine vinegar and caster sugar in a bowl, stirring until the sugar has dissolved. Add the carrot and cucumber ribbons, cover and set aside for 30 minutes to pickle.

2. Bring a saucepan of salted water to the boil and cook the red cabbage for 5 minutes. Strain the cabbage over a large measuring jug, reserving the blue cooking water.

3. Add the rice to the now-empty saucepan and pour over 300 ml (½ pint) of the blue cabbage water. Return the saucepan to the hob, over a very low heat. Cover and cook for 25 minutes.

4. Once the rice is cooked and has turned purple, having absorbed all the coloured water, spread it across a plate to cool.

5. Squeeze the lime juice over the cooled rice. The areas hit by the lime juice will turn a bright pink, giving the rice a purple-and-pink tie-dyed effect!

6. Now construct the unicorn bowls. Divide the rice between 2 cereal bowls. Top each with a small handful of red cabbage. Drain and rinse the pickled veg ribbons under cold water, then arrange them around the edges of the bowls. Finish with the slices of avocado and a small handful of vegan cheese puffs for that all-important crunch!

7. In a small bowl, combine the vegan mayo and sriracha. Drizzle this over the bowls, then scatter over the coriander and sesame seeds and serve.

PREP TIME: **10 MINUTES**

COOK TIME: **1 HOUR**

DIFFICULTY: **EASY**

SERVES: **4**

MEAT

CHEESY SHEPHERD'S PIE POTATO SKINS

You lot know we have to take a British classic and put that Snackin' finesse on it! Shepherd's pie loaded in crispy potato skins with bare melted cheeeeese.

INGREDIENTS

4 large baking potatoes

2 tablespoons vegetable oil

½ onion, finely chopped

2 garlic cloves, very finely chopped

1 carrot, finely chopped

300 g (10½ oz) minced lamb

2 teaspoons Worcestershire sauce

large handful of frozen peas

25 g (1 oz) salted butter

50 g (1¾ oz) finely grated Cheddar cheese

25 g (1 oz) cheese-flavoured corn chips, crushed

salt and pepper

steamed greens, to serve

METHOD

1. Preheat the oven to 190°C (375°F), Gas Mark 5.

2. Using a sharp knife, prick each potato 4–5 times; this will allow any steam to escape during baking. Wrap the potatoes in foil and bake for 50 minutes, or simply microwave on high (without foil) for 10 minutes, turning after 5 minutes.

3. Meanwhile, heat the oil in a large frying pan over a low-medium heat and sweat the onion, garlic and carrot until softened.

4. Increase the heat to medium–high and add the minced lamb, breaking it up with a wooden spoon as it cooks. Brown the lamb for 8-10 minutes, then add a splash of water, along with the Worcestershire sauce, and some salt and pepper. Reduce the heat and gently simmer for 20 minutes.

5. Stir the frozen peas through the lamb mixture.

6. Remove the baked potatoes from the oven and slice in half. Spoon out their centres into a large mixing bowl. Combine the fluffy potato with the butter, Cheddar and a pinch of salt and pepper.

7. Spoon the lamb mince into each potato skin. Top with the cheesy mash, then sprinkle over the crushed corn chips. Return to the oven for 10 minutes until golden on top.

8. Allow to cool a little before serving with a side of steamed greens.

FISH FINGER KATSU CURRY

PREP TIME: **15 MINUTES**

COOK TIME: **15 MINUTES**

DIFFICULTY: **EASY**

SERVES: **2**

FISH

Need I say more? Flaky fish fingers finessed with that aromatic creamy katsu curry. Vibes for days.

INGREDIENTS

6 fish fingers

For the curry sauce

1 tablespoon vegetable oil

½ onion, finely chopped

75 g (2¾ oz) carrot, diced

2 garlic cloves, very finely chopped

1 teaspoon peeled and finely grated fresh root ginger

1 teaspoon garam masala

½ teaspoon ground turmeric

2 tablespoons honey

1 tablespoon soy sauce

400 ml (14 fl oz) vegetable stock

120 g (4¼ oz) jasmine rice

salt and pepper

To serve (all optional)

coriander

sesame seeds

baby spinach leaves

Butterhead lettuce leaves

raw carrot ribbons

METHOD

1. Preheat the oven to 230°C (450°F), Gas Mark 8. Place the fish fingers on an oven tray and cook for 12 minutes.

2. Meanwhile, heat the oil in a frying pan over a low-medium heat and sweat the onion, carrot, garlic and ginger with the garam masala and turmeric.

3. After 5 minutes, stir in the honey and soy sauce and pour over the stock. Increase the heat and bring the sauce to the boil, then reduce the heat and simmer for 10 minutes, or until the sauce has thickened. If you prefer a smoother sauce, use a stick blender to blitz the sauce to a silky consistency. Taste and season accordingly.

4. Meanwhile, cook the rice according to the packet instructions.

5. Serve the fish fingers with a mound of rice and the katsu curry sauce generously spooned over the top. Sprinkle with coriander leaves and sesame seeds, if you like, or serve with a side salad for added colour.

TIP:
After a veggie option? See the Veggie Katsu Curry on page 177.

TOAD-IN-THE-HOLE LOAF

Who needs plain old bread when you can have this BANGER in loaf form! British comfort food served to your headtop.

INGREDIENTS

8 pork sausages

250 g (9 oz) plain flour

2 teaspoons mustard powder

½ teaspoon salt

3 eggs

175 ml (6 fl oz) whole milk

45 ml (3 tablespoons) vegetable oil

caramelised red onion gravy and mixed veg, to serve (optional)

METHOD

1. Preheat the oven to 220°C (425°F), Gas Mark 7.

2. Sift the flour, mustard powder and salt into a large mixing bowl, then add the eggs and beat to combine. Once you have a smooth, thick mixture, gradually whisk in the milk until a loose batter forms. Cover and place in the refrigerator for 15 minutes to chill.

3. Meanwhile, lay the sausages along the base of a loaf tin and bake for 10 minutes until lightly browned.

4. Remove the loaf tin from the oven. Take out the sausages and set aside, then pour the vegetable oil into the base of the tin and return to the oven for 3 minutes to heat the oil.

5. When the oil is hot, pour in the chilled batter and add the sausages – they will sink into the batter a little. Carefully return the tin to the oven for 30–35 minutes. Do not open the oven door during this time, or the batter may fail to rise, or collapse. After this time, the batter should have fluffed out with a golden crust and the sausages should be a deep golden brown.

6. Allow to cool a little, then turn out on to a board and slice into portions.

7. Serve with onion gravy and mixed veg for the perfect dinner!

CHEESE HAT CHILLI

PREP TIME: **10 MINUTES**
COOK TIME: **30 MINUTES**
DIFFICULTY: **EASY**
SERVES: **4**
VEGAN

Cheeeeeeeese hat chilli. Hearty sweet and potato flavaaas tucked underneath a crispy cheese hat.

INGREDIENTS

2 tablespoons olive oil

1 onion, finely chopped

2 garlic cloves, very finely chopped

1 large sweet potato, peeled and chopped

400 g (14 oz) can of chopped tomatoes

400 ml (14 fl oz) vegetable stock

400 g (14 oz) can of red kidney beans, drained

400 g (14 oz) can of black beans, drained

1 teaspoon chilli powder

1 teaspoon smoked paprika

1 teaspoon ground cumin

1 teaspoon cocoa powder

250 g (9 oz) grated vegan cheese

2 jalapeños, sliced

salt and pepper

long-grain rice, avocado and coriander, to serve (optional)

METHOD

1. Heat the oil in a large, deep ovenproof frying pan over a medium heat and sweat the onion, garlic and sweet potato.

2. Once the vegetables have started to soften (around 10 minutes), add the canned tomatoes, stock, beans, spices and cocoa, and season with salt and pepper. Stir everything through and simmer over a low heat for 20 minutes until the sauce has reduced.

3. Preheat the grill to medium.

4. Top the chilli with the vegan cheese in a generous layer and scatter over the sliced jalapeños. Place under the grill for 10 minutes, until the cheese starts to melt, bubble and crisp up.

5. Dive into the cheesy crust and serve in bowls. Enjoy as it is, or with long-grain rice, avocado and coriander.

ONE-TRAY TANDOORI SUNDAY ROAST

Top your roast chicken and veggies with that flames tandoori twist! All in one tray for EASE. You're welcome. Careful here that your chicken is cooked: give it 45 minutes per 1 kg (2 lb 4 oz) and work out how long yours needs by weighing it before you cook it.

INGREDIENTS

For the quick curry paste

3 teaspoons garam masala

3 teaspoons chilli powder

1 teaspoon salt

2 tablespoons garlic paste

2 tablespoons unsalted butter, at room temperature

6 tablespoons olive oil

For the chicken and vegetables

1 large high-welfare chicken (roughly 1.9 kg/4 lb 4 oz)

1 kg (2 lb 4 oz) new potatoes

3 large carrots, cut into chunky batons

1 head of broccoli, cut into large florets

500 ml (19 fl oz) chicken stock

All in one tray for EASE. You're welcome.

METHOD

1. Preheat the oven to 200°C (400°F), Gas Mark 6. In a small bowl, combine the curry paste ingredients until smooth. Weigh your chicken and calculate its cooking time (see recipe introduction).

2. Place a wire rack over a large, deep roasting tin and lay the chicken on top. Smooth half of the curry paste over the chicken, ensuring it is evenly coated. Cover the chicken with foil and transfer to the oven.

3. Put the vegetables into a large bowl and spoon over the remaining curry paste. Massage the veg with your hands, ensuring they are well coated. Cover and set aside.

4. After 50 minutes, remove the chicken from the oven. Remove the foil, carefully lift the wire rack off the roasting tin and set the chicken aside. Tip any juices from the roasting tin into a small bowl or mug. Lay the vegetables across the base of the roasting tin and rest the wire rack with the chicken back on top.

5. Pour the juices over the chicken to baste it, then return to the oven for 35 minutes, or as long as your calculation told you, until the vegetables and chicken are cooked through and the chicken skin is golden and crisp. If the chicken skin starts to catch or burn at any point, cover it with foil.

6. Remove the chicken and veg from the oven. Insert a skewer into the thickest part of the chicken breast to check it is cooked through – the skewer should come out piping hot and the juices from the meat should run clear. Transfer the chicken to a board to rest for at least 15 minutes and spoon the vegetables into a heated serving dish, leaving any juices in the tin. Cover the chicken and veggies with foil to keep in the heat.

7. Place the roasting tin on the hob over a low-medium heat. Once the juices start to bubble, pour in a large splash of stock. Bring to a simmer and, using a wooden spoon, scrape the tin to loosen any residue. Pour in the rest of the stock and increase the heat a little. Allow the gravy to simmer and reduce for 15 minutes.

8. Carve the chicken and serve up with the veggies and a generous ladle of tandoori–infused gravy. Tuck in!

DIY CHICKEN SHAWARMA KEBABS

PREP TIME: **10 MINUTES +
  MARINATING**

COOK TIME: **1 HOUR**

DIFFICULTY: **EASY**

SERVES: **4**

MEAT

**Be your own boss(man) and whip up our
mouth-watering chicken shawarma kebabs.
Go all out with juicy marinated chicken,
flatbread, veggies... the full works.**

INGREDIENTS

For the marinade

150 g (5½ oz) plain yogurt

2 teaspoons chilli powder

2 teaspoons garam masala

1 teaspoon salt

1 tablespoon garlic paste

1 tablespoon Dijon mustard

juice of ½ lemon

For the kebabs

8 skinless, boneless chicken
thighs

1 large onion, peeled

8 flatbread wraps

mixed salad (cucumbers,
tomatoes, carrot, red
cabbage, lettuce)

4 tablespoons harissa
mayonnaise

METHOD

1. In a large bowl, combine the marinade ingredients
    and add the chicken thighs, ensuring they are well
    coated. Cover and place in the refrigerator for at
    least 30 minutes, or overnight, to marinate.

2. Remove from the refrigerator and allow to come
    to room temperature. Meanwhile, soak 3 wooden
    skewers in a bowl of water.

3. Preheat the oven to 180°C (350°F), Gas Mark 4.

4. Slice the onion in half and place one half, flat–side
    down, in the centre of a baking tray. Push 2 skewers
    vertically into the onion, one on the left and one on
    the right. Slide the chicken thighs down the skewers
    so both skewers pierce each thigh, layering them up,
    one on top of the other. Carefully slide a third skewer
    down through the middle of the chicken and onion for
    added support, making sure it, too, pierces each thigh.
    Top with the second onion half, flat–side down, to hold
    the skewers in place.

5. Transfer to the oven (ensure there is enough space
    for the construction to stand upright) and cook for
    1 hour until the chicken is cooked through, compact
    and golden with caramelised edges.

6. Remove from the oven and allow to rest for 10 minutes
    before serving.

7. Slice the chicken vertically and serve in flatbreads,
    over a bed of mixed salad. Finish with a generous
    drizzle of harissa mayonnaise and enjoy!

CHILLI BEEF MOODLES

PREP TIME: **10 MINUTES**
COOK TIME: **15 MINUTES**
DIFFICULTY: **EASY**
SERVES: **4**
MEAT

Imagine a bowl full of noodz with crispy caramelised beef mince, fresh veggies, a chilli oil kick, a little sweet honey and salty soy. OOOOOFT.

INGREDIENTS

1 tablespoon vegetable oil

4 spring onions, sliced

2 garlic cloves, very finely chopped

4 red chillies, sliced (seeds in or out, depending on spice preference)

500 g (1 lb 2 oz) minced beef

2 carrots, sliced into fine matchsticks

2 heads of pak choi, sliced

4 tablespoons soy sauce

3 tablespoons honey

2 tablespoons hot chilli sauce

225 g (8 oz) cooked flat rice noodles

sesame seeds and coriander, to serve (optional)

METHOD

1. Heat the vegetable oil in a large frying pan over a medium heat and soften the spring onions, garlic and chillies. Increase the heat to high and add the minced beef, breaking it up with a wooden spoon as it cooks. Fry for 10 minutes, or until browned.

2. Add the carrots, pak choi, soy sauce, honey and chilli sauce. Stir-fry for a further 5 minutes, until the veg is al dente and the beef is crispy and starting to caramelise in the sauces.

3. Remove from the heat and toss through the flat rice noodles, ensuring they are well coated in the sauce and crispy beef.

4. Divide the noodles between 4 warmed bowls and serve, topped with sesame seeds and coriander, if you like.

CAUGHT
FAKIN'

CAUGHT QUIZ

WHICH CAUGHT CHEF ARE YOU?

Listen, if you have this cookbook, you're in the gang, but obviously we have to see what sort of chefileeni you are. Take this quiz and find out.

Yes, my G.

You like cooking for the gang?

I always have the mandem over.

You best know my food is for ME.

Have you got people asking you for chefileeni wisdom?

Keeping my hacks to myself.

Do people vibe with you while you chef it up?

I'm a guru, fam.

I'm cheffing up good vibes only.

The only thing I'm vibing with is my food.

How patterned is your fridge?

My shelves are STACKED.

I'm hitting up the shop every time.

Gang every time.

BOUJEE CHEF

IS THAT YOU YEAH? Sorry we don't cook with golden spatulas like you fam. Get yourself a palace and swim in gold.

CHILL CHEF

If you're chill, then you are defo a part of the Caught Snackin' GANG! Come through to the TikTok HQ and grab an apron, I'm tired.

START

Do you follow recipes when you chef it up?

Bless with freestyle.

Time for munch, is it a sit-down ting or keeping it casual?

Here for them fancy dinners.

Sofa VIBES.

Are you one of them 'all the gear, no idea'?

Have you ever done a madness in the kitchen? (Flames, danger, floods 'n' that.)

I got both.

I can't lie...

Nope all safe here, G.

You lot googling ingredients before a shop?

Got that fire extinguisher ready.

Nah.

Deleting my search history

You running solo or you cheffing with the gang?

Are people really eating your food tho?

Solo shubz.

Mandem can't get enough.

No comment.

STRESS CHEF

I appreciate you stressin' just means you care, but don't come at me with your bad vibes and energies, chef.

DEAD CHEF

If you've reached this point, you may as well go to bed. You can't handle it. Just drink water, innit. It's a takeaway ting for you, G.

A molten mozzarella middle for the mandem

CHEESY GARLIC-BUTTER DOUGH BALLS

PREP TIME: **10 MINUTES**

COOK TIME: **25 MINUTES**

DIFFICULTY: **EASY**

SERVES: **2** (as a snack or starter, makes around 10)

VEGGIE

These DECADENT garlic-'bootah' balls are stuffed with a molten mozzarella middle for the mandem.

INGREDIENTS

100 g (3½ oz) salted butter, at room temperature

2 tablespoons finely chopped parsley leaves

3 garlic cloves, very finely chopped

180 g (6 oz) self-raising flour, plus more to dust

1 teaspoon salt

180 g (6 oz) Greek-style yogurt

10 mozzarella cheese pearls, drained and patted dry with kitchen paper

METHOD

1. Preheat the oven to 180°C (350°F), Gas Mark 4. Line a baking tray with nonstick baking paper.

2. In a medium-sized bowl, combine the butter, parsley and garlic. Put half the garlic butter mix in a small saucepan and gently melt over a low heat.

3. Sift the flour into a large bowl and add the salt and yogurt. Roughly bring the ingredients together with a wooden spoon or spatula, then go in with your hands and shape the mixture into a ball. Transfer to a lightly floured surface. Knead for a couple of minutes until you have a smooth, firm dough.

4. Divide the dough into 10 balls. Flatten the balls and place a mozzarella pearl in the centre of each one, then shape the dough around the mozzarella, pressing the edges together to seal. Lay the dough balls across the prepared tray and brush with the melted garlic butter.

5. Bake for 20 minutes, or until golden and melting in the middle.

6. Serve with the remaining garlic butter, melted, for dipping.

VEGGIE KATSU CURRY

PREP TIME: **15 MINUTES**

COOK TIME: **45 MINUTES**

DIFFICULTY: **EASY**

SERVES: **2**

VEGGIE

Katsu curry will always be a personal fave and this veggie version is no joke! Douse golden slices of panko-coated aubergine in creamy katsu sauce and don't look back.

INGREDIENTS

125g (4½ oz) panko breadcrumbs

75g (2¾ oz) plain flour

2 eggs, lightly beaten

1 large aubergine, sliced into thick rounds

1 quantity katsu curry sauce (see page 157)

250g (9 oz) jasmine rice (cooked weight), to serve

salt and pepper

To serve (optional)

coriander leaves

sesame seeds

fresh veg salad

METHOD

1. Preheat the oven to 200°C (400°F), Gas Mark 6.

2. Pour the panko breadcrumbs out across a baking tray and toast in the oven for 8–10 minutes until pale golden. Remove from the oven and allow to cool for 10 minutes or so. Leave the oven on.

3. Put the flour, eggs and toasted panko crumbs into 3 separate bowls. Generously season the flour with salt and pepper, then turn the aubergine slices in it, ensuring they are evenly coated. Tap off any excess flour, then dip the aubergine slices in the egg, followed by the toasted crumbs.

4. Lay the coated aubergine slices across a wire rack set over an oven tray and bake for 30–35 minutes until golden and crisp with soft centres.

5. Meanwhile, make the katsu sauce.

6. Remove the aubergine slices from the oven and serve with jasmine rice, with the katsu sauce generously spooned over. Scatter with coriander and sesame seeds, and eat with a fresh veg salad, if you like.

PREP TIME: **10 MINUTES**

COOK TIME: **35 MINUTES**

DIFFICULTY: **EASY**

SERVES: **2**

MEAT

PERI PERI CHICKEN BURGER

Thought you knew where to get your favourite peri peri chicken? THINK AGAIN. Make your own at home and turn the flames dial UP.

INGREDIENTS

For the burgers

2 skinless, boneless chicken thighs

2 tablespoons mayonnaise

2 soft white burger buns

2 Cheddar cheese slices

4 large lettuce leaves

50 g (1¾ oz) shop-bought coleslaw

1 large tomato, sliced (optional)

½ red onion, sliced (optional)

For the peri peri sauce

1 red pepper, roughly chopped

1 red chilli, deseeded

1 garlic clove

2 teaspoons smoked paprika

2 tablespoons olive oil

METHOD

1. Preheat the oven to 200°C (400°F), Gas Mark 6.

2. Start with the sauce. Put the red pepper, chilli, garlic, paprika and olive oil in a blender and blitz to form a smooth sauce.

3. Lay the chicken thighs flat in a shallow bowl or dish. Pour three-quarters of the sauce over them, ensuring they are well coated. Combine the remaining sauce with the mayonnaise to make a peri peri mayo.

4. Toast the buns in a frying pan over a medium-high heat for 2-3 minutes.

5. Fry the chicken thighs in the same pan over a high heat for 5 minutes on each side until charred. Transfer them to the oven and cook for a further 20 minutes. In the final 5 minutes of cooking time, top each thigh with a slice of Cheddar cheese and allow to melt.

6. Spread the buns with peri peri mayo, then fill with lettuce, coleslaw, tomato and onion slices (if you like), along with the juicy, cheesy chicken thighs.

GIN & TONIC FISH & CHIPS

PREP TIME: **15 MINUTES +**
  CHILLING

COOK TIME: **30 MINUTES**

DIFFICULTY: **ADVANCED**

SERVES: **2**

FISH

These bougie, boozy battered fillets will have you turnt for fish friday! Finessed with crispy, chunky chips and mushy peas OBVS.

INGREDIENTS

For the batter

100 g (3½ oz) plain flour, plus more to lightly coat the fish

½ teaspoon salt

150 ml (5 fl oz) tonic water

25 ml (1 fl oz) gin

For the fish and chips

300 g (10½ oz) frozen thick-cut oven chips

500 ml (18 fl oz) vegetable oil

2 haddock or cod fillets, about 140 g (5 oz) each

To serve

tartare sauce

lemon wedges

mushy peas

TIP:
The bubbles in the tonic make for an extra crunchy, light batter. No tonic? Use sparkling water instead.

METHOD

1. Preheat the oven to 220°C (425°F), Gas Mark 7.

2. Put the flour and salt into a medium-sized bowl and gradually pour in the tonic water, stirring until you have a smooth batter. Add the gin and stir through. Cover and chill in the refrigerator for at least 20 minutes.

3. Lay out the oven chips across a large oven tray and bake for 15-20 minutes, or according to the packet instructions.

4. Pour the vegetable oil into a large, deep saucepan with a well-fitting lid and set over a medium heat until it reaches 180°C (350°F). (See page 17 for deep-frying hacks.)

5. When the batter has sufficiently chilled, remove from the refrigerator. Pat dry the fish fillets with kitchen roll and turn them in plain flour to lightly coat, then dip them in the batter, ensuring they are evenly coated.

6. When the oil has reached 180°C (350°F), carefully add the battered fillets and fry for 5-7 minutes, until golden, crisp and cooked through. Remove the fillets from the oil and place on a plate double-lined with kitchen paper to drain off any excess oil.

7. Serve the battered fish with the chunky chips, tartare sauce, lemon wedges and mushy peas.

MIGHTY MEATBALL SUB

PREP TIME: **15 MINUTES**
COOK TIME: **30 MINUTES**
DIFFICULTY: **EASY**
SERVES: **2**
MEAT

Our big boi meatball sub will fill the heart, soul and stomach for DAYS.

INGREDIENTS

For the meatballs

1 tablespoon olive oil

¼ onion, grated

2 garlic cloves, very finely chopped

125 g (4½ oz) minced beef

125 g (4½ oz) minced pork

1 teaspoon Italian mixed dried herbs

1 tablespoon finely grated Parmesan cheese

1 egg, lightly beaten

salt and pepper

For the sub

200 g (7 oz) shop–bought tomato and basil sauce

¼ teaspoon chilli flakes

2 small baguettes or sub rolls

6 mozzarella cheese slices

2 basil sprigs

METHOD

1. Preheat the oven to 190°C (375°F), Gas Mark 5.

2. Heat the olive oil in a large frying pan over a low heat and sweat the onion and garlic for 5 minutes until softened.

3. Transfer to a medium–sized bowl and combine with the beef, pork, dried herbs, Parmesan and egg, and season with salt and pepper.

4. Divide the mixture into 10 balls and lay across a baking tray. Bake for 15 minutes until golden and cooked through. After 15 minutes, remove the meatballs from the oven and preheat the grill to medium.

5. Meanwhile, pour the tomato and basil sauce into the frying pan you used for the onions and bring to a gentle simmer over a low-medium heat. Add the baked meatballs and sprinkle with the chilli flakes, then cover and simmer for 10–15 minutes until the sauce has thickened.

6. Halve the baguettes or subs lengthways. Divide the meatballs between them and spoon over the tomato sauce. Top with the mozzarella slices and basil and place under the grill for 3–5 minutes, until the cheese is melted and bubbling. Enjoy immediately.

PLANT BURGER WITH SECRET SAUCE

PREP TIME: **10 MINUTES**

COOK TIME: **20 MINUTES**

DIFFICULTY: **EASY**

SERVES: **2**

VEGAN

LISTEN, don't say we don't spoil you guys when we're out here dishing out our Caught SECRET sauce that slaps with this plant burger. Keep this between us, yeah? Safe.

INGREDIENTS

For the burger sauce

2 tablespoons vegan mayonnaise

1 tablespoon tomato ketchup

1 tablespoon sriracha

1 tablespoon American mustard

1 tablespoon cornichons, finely chopped (optional)

salt and pepper

For the burgers

1 tbsp olive oil

½ red onion, sliced into rounds

2 vegan burgers

2 vegan burger cheese slices

2 brioche burger buns, halved

1 head of curly leaf lettuce

1 large tomato, sliced

METHOD

1. In a small bowl, combine the burger sauce ingredients. Taste and season accordingly with salt and pepper.

2. Heat the oil in a frying pan over a low-medium heat and sweat the onion for 10 minutes or so, until soft and caramelised. Transfer to a small bowl.

3. In the same pan, fry the burgers according to the packet instructions. In the final minute of cooking, add a slice of cheese to the top of each one. Set the burgers aside while you toast the buns in the same frying pan.

4. Generously spread the toasted buns with burger sauce and layer up with curly lettuce leaves, tomato slices, a burger with melting cheese and the sweet caramelised onions. Top with a burger–bun lid and enjoy immediately.

FRIED CHICKEN BUCKET

When the mandem roll through, best know this crispy, succulent fried chicken bucket will have them feeling satisfied. You will make a lot of friends with this bucket... you heard it here first.

INGREDIENTS

For the seasoned flour

600 g (1 lb 5 oz) plain flour

4 teaspoons Italian mixed dried herbs

4 teaspoons chilli powder

4 teaspoons hot paprika

4 teaspoons garlic powder

4 teaspoons onion powder

2 teaspoons pepper

4 teaspoons salt

For the fried chicken

4 eggs, lightly beaten

600 ml (20 fl oz) natural yogurt or buttermilk

1 litre (1¾ pints) vegetable or sunflower oil, to deep–fry

1 kg (2 lb 4 oz) skinless, boneless chicken thighs

1 kg (2 lb 4 oz) skinless, boneless chicken drumsticks

To serve (optional)

grilled sweetcorn cobettes

baked beans

chips

METHOD

1. Combine the seasoned flour ingredients in a medium–sized bowl.

2. Whisk the egg and yogurt or buttermilk in a separate bowl.

3. Pour the oil into a large, deep saucepan with a well–fitting lid and set over a medium heat. (See page 17 for deep–frying hacks.) Preheat the oven to 120°C (250°F), Gas Mark ½.

4. Pat dry all of the chicken thighs and drumsticks with kitchen paper. Dip them in the egg mixture and then the seasoned flour. Repeat to double–coat the chicken, for extra crunch!

5. When the oil has reached 180°C (350°F), cook the coated chicken in batches for 15 minutes, until golden, super crisp and cooked through. Drain off any excess oil on a plate double–lined with kitchen paper. Spread out the cooked chicken on a baking tray and keep warm in the oven while you cook the rest.

6. Serve the chicken pieces, piled high, with sweetcorn, beans and chips on the side.

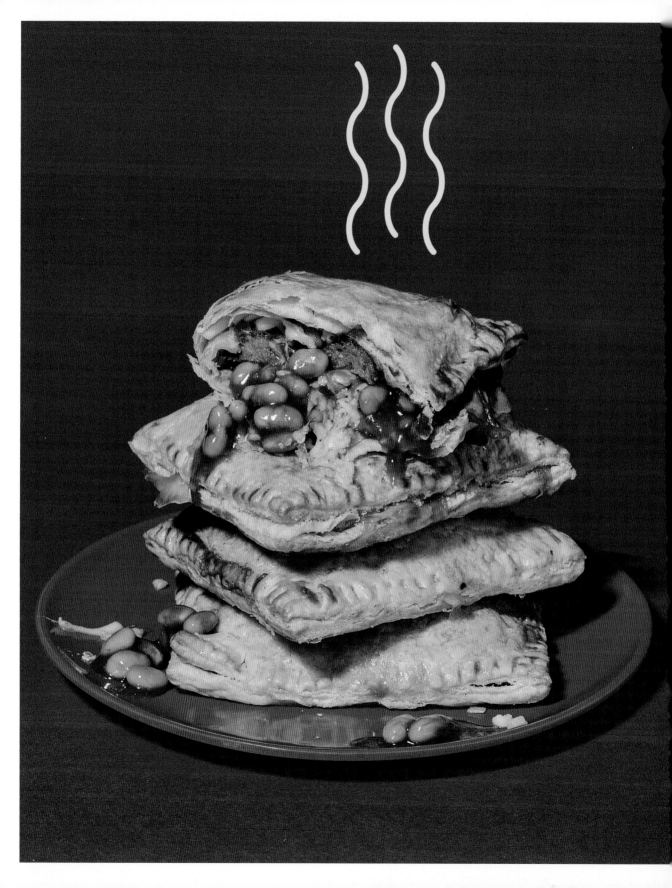

MEATLESS BEAN & CHEEZ MELTS

PREP TIME: **15 MINUTES**
COOK TIME: **40 MINUTES**
DIFFICULTY: **EASY**
SERVES: **4**
VEGAN

This baked goodie is a sensational crowd-pleaser: hot puff-pastry pockets of melted cheese, baked beans and veggie sausage.

INGREDIENTS

4 vegan sausages

500 g (1 lb 2 oz) block of vegan puff pastry

2 tablespoons plain flour, to dust

8 tablespoons baked beans

75 g (2¾ oz) grated vegan Cheddar-style cheese

90 g (3¼ oz) vegan, non-dairy spread, melted

METHOD

1. Preheat the oven to 190°C (375°F), Gas Mark 5 and line a baking tray with nonstick baking paper.

2. Lay the sausages across a baking tray and cook in the oven for 15 minutes, or according to the packet instructions. Allow them to cool, then halve lengthways. Leave the oven on.

3. Roll out the pastry on a lightly floured surface and cut it into 4 even rectangles. Position one of the pieces of pastry with a long side facing you and top the right-hand side with 2 tablespoons of baked beans, 2 sausage halves and a handful of grated cheese, leaving a border around the edge.

4. Brush the borders of the pastry with the melted spread.

5. Fold the left side of the pastry over the filling so the edges meet. Crimp with a fork to seal the pastry and score the top with a sharp knife. Repeat to make the other 3 parcels.

6. Arrange the pastries on the prepared tray. Brush with more melted spread and then bake for 25 minutes until golden and puffed up. Allow to cool for 5 minutes before serving.

GLAZED VANILLA DOUGHNUTS

PREP TIME: **10 MINUTES +**
CHILLING
COOK TIME: **12 MINUTES**
DIFFICULTY: **EASY**
SERVES: **2**
VEGGIE

When Homer Simpson said, 'Mmmmmmm.... doughnuts,' best believe he was referencing these.

INGREDIENTS

160 g (5¾ oz) self-raising flour

80 g (2¾ oz) caster sugar

200 g (7 oz) full-fat natural yogurt

500 ml (18 fl oz) vegetable or sunflower oil

250 g (9 oz) icing sugar

75 ml (5 tablespoons) milk

1 teaspoon vanilla extract

rainbow sprinkles (optional)

METHOD

1. In a medium-sized bowl, combine the flour, sugar and yogurt until you have a smooth, thick mixture. Cover and chill in the refrigerator for 15 minutes.

2. Heat the oil, in a large, deep saucepan with a well-fitting lid, to 180°C (350°F). (See page 17 for deep-frying hacks.)

3. Use an ice-cream scoop to carefully scoop portions of the chilled batter into the hot oil. Fry in batches for 5-6 minutes, until golden and cooked through with a dense yet fluffy centre. These doughnuts have a delicious cakey texture!

4. Remove the doughnuts from the oil and drain off the excess oil on a plate double-lined with kitchen paper.

5. Meanwhile, make the glaze by combining the icing sugar, milk and vanilla extract in a shallow bowl.

6. Roll the doughnuts in the glaze and lay them out across a wire rack for about 15 minutes, or until the glaze has set. Enjoy as they are, or top with rainbow sprinkles to serve.

TIP:
Skewer a hole in the doughnuts and squeeze in chocolate sauce to level up.

FAKE IT ICED MOCHA

Who wants to queue to have some MEADY coffee? With this tasty caffeinated bevi, you'll become a barista in your own kitchen! Lightwork.

INGREDIENTS

2 large handfuls of ice cubes

2 shots of freshly brewed espresso

250 ml (9 fl oz) chilled milk (dairy or plant–based)

1 tablespoon chocolate syrup, plus more to serve

1 teaspoon granulated sugar

aerosol can of squirty cream, to serve

METHOD

1. Wrap half of the ice cubes in a clean tea towel and bash with a rolling pin to crush into small pieces.

2. Put the crushed ice into a blender with the espresso, milk, chocolate syrup and sugar. Blend for 30 seconds, until well combined.

3. Pour into tall glasses over the remaining ice cubes. Top with squirty cream and a drizzle of chocolate syrup and get slurpin'.

CAUGHT BAKIN'

2- OR 3-INGREDIENT BAKES

You know them lazy days, but you're craving them SWEET ONES? These simple bakes will pattern you.

2-INGREDIENT

CHOCOLATE COOKIES

PREP TIME: **2 MINUTES**

COOK TIME: **10 MINUTES**

DIFFICULTY: **EASY**

MAKES: **10–12**

VEGGIE

INGREDIENTS

200 g (7 oz) chocolate hazelnut spread, such as Nutella

75 g (2¾ oz) plain flour

METHOD

1. Preheat the oven to 180°C (350°F), Gas Mark 4. Line a baking tray with nonstick baking paper.

2. Combine the Nutella and flour in a large bowl until you have a thick, smooth mixture.

3. Divide and roll the mixture into even-sized balls and lay these across the prepared tray.

4. Gently squash each ball a little with a teaspoon and bake the cookies for 10 minutes, until cooked through with a cakey consistency.

5. Allow to cool a little before serving.

CHOCOLATE SOUFFLÉ

PREP TIME: **10 MINUTES**

COOK TIME: **15–20 MINUTES**

DIFFICULTY: **EASY**

SERVES: **2**

VEGGIE

INGREDIENTS

150 g (5½ oz) chocolate hazelnut
spread, such as Nutella

2 eggs, separated

METHOD

1. Preheat the oven to 190°C (375°F), Gas Mark 5.

2. Whisk the egg yolks in a medium–sized bowl. Add the Nutella and stir until you have a smooth paste.

3. Whisk the egg whites in another medium–sized bowl for about 2 minutes until holding their shape.

4. Fold the egg whites through the Nutella mixture. Pour into 2 ramekins, leaving about 1cm (½ inch) at the top.

5. Bake for 15–20 minutes until fluffed up and cooked on the outside with a soft, melting centre. Do not open the oven door while baking, or the soufflé won't rise. Serve immediately.

CHOCOLATE MOUSSE

PREP TIME: **10 MINUTES**

COOK TIME: **NONE**

DIFFICULTY: **EASY**

SERVES: **2**

VEGAN

INGREDIENTS

200 g (7 oz) dark chocolate

150 ml (¼ pint) just–boiled water

250 g (9 oz) ice cubes

METHOD

1. Break the chocolate into small pieces in a medium heatproof bowl and pour over the measured water. Stir until the chocolate has completely melted into the water.

2. Set the bowl over another larger bowl containing the ice cubes and whisk the chocolate mixture, using an electric whisk, for 2-3 minutes, until thick and fluffy.

3. Spoon into 2 individual glasses and serve immediately, or keep in the refrigerator for later. These will keep in the refrigerator for up to 3 days.

3-INGREDIENT

CRÈME BRÛLÉE

PREP TIME: **5 MINUTES + CHILLING**
COOK TIME: **30 MINUTES**
DIFFICULTY: **EASY**
SERVES: **4**
VEGGIE

INGREDIENTS

480 ml (17 fl oz) tub of vanilla ice cream, melted
4 egg yolks
4 tablespoons granulated sugar

METHOD

1. Place a deep oven tray or dish in the oven. Preheat the oven to 170°C (340°F), Gas Mark 3½ and fill and boil the kettle.

2. Whisk together the melted ice cream and egg yolks until combined and pour this into 4 ovenproof ramekins.

3. Place the ramekins in the hot oven tray. Pour in just-boiled water from the kettle so that it comes three-quarters of the way up the sides of the ramekins.

4. Bake for 25-30 minutes, then remove the ramekins from the tray. The crème should have a firm jiggle to it when tapped. Cover the ramekins and place them in the refrigerator to cool.

5. Once cool, sprinkle over a layer of granulated sugar. Preheat the grill to medium and grill until the sugar has melted to a deep golden brown. Allow the sugar to cool, then place in the refrigerator for 30 minutes to set, or until you are ready to serve. These will keep in the refrigerator for up to 3 days.

These simple bakes will pattern you

CHOCOLATE ICE CREAM CAKE

PREP TIME: **5 MINUTES**

COOK TIME: **35–40 MINUTES**

DIFFICULTY: **EASY**

SERVES: **8**

VEGGIE

INGREDIENTS

480 ml (17 fl oz) tub of chocolate ice cream, melted

175 g (6 oz) self-raising flour

150 g (5½ oz) milk chocolate chips

METHOD

1. Preheat the oven to 180°C (350°F), Gas Mark 4. Line a 900g (2lb) loaf tin with nonstick baking paper.

2. Mix the melted ice cream and self-raising flour in a large bowl until smooth and well combined.

3. Fold through the chocolate chips and pour the mixture into the prepared tin.

4. Bake for 35-40 minutes, or until a skewer inserted into the middle comes out clean.

5. Allow to cool in the tin, then turn out and slice to serve.

VANILLA CUPCAKES

PREP TIME: **5 MINUTES**

COOK TIME: **20–25 MINUTES**

DIFFICULTY: **EASY**

MAKES: **6–8**

VEGGIE

INGREDIENTS

245 g (8¾ oz) packet of vanilla cake mix

245 ml (9 fl oz) full-fat mayonnaise

400 g (14 oz) tub of vanilla icing

METHOD

1. Preheat the oven to 180°C (350°F), Gas Mark 4. Line a muffin tin with 6-8 cupcake cases.

2. Combine the cake mix and mayonnaise in a large bowl until smooth.

3. Distribute the cake mixture evenly between the prepared cupcake cases.

4. Bake for 20-25 minutes, or until cooked through, then remove the cupcakes from the tin and allow to cool on a wire rack. Top with shop-bought icing and enjoy.

CHOCOLATE MUG CAKE

Don't be a mug; try this cake.

INGREDIENTS

30 g (1 oz) salted butter, at room temperature

50 g (1¾ oz) caster sugar

3 tablespoons boiling water

2 tablespoons cocoa powder

35 g (1¼ oz) self–raising flour

¼ teaspoon salt

1 tablespoon chocolate chips

METHOD

1. Put the butter, caster sugar and measured boiling water in a microwaveable mug and stir until melted.

2. Add the cocoa powder, flour and salt and stir through until well combined and smooth.

3. Fold in the chocolate chips and microwave on high (or at 900W) for 1 minute 15 seconds, or until baked on top with a soft, gooey centre. Dig in with a spoon!

TIP:
Prep these in advance and refrigerate. Just chuck them in the microwave when ready to serve.

GIANT PAN COOKIE

PREP TIME: **10 MINUTES**
COOK TIME: **12 MINUTES**
DIFFICULTY: **EASY**
SERVES: **4**
VEGGIE

Gooey cookies are good and that. But one in GIANT form? Oozing all over the place, on my plate, on your plate? It's great, just make it.

INGREDIENTS

120 g (4¼ oz) unsalted butter, plus more for the pan

50 g (1¾ oz) light brown sugar

50 g (1¾ oz) caster sugar

1 egg, plus 1 egg yolk

1 teaspoon vanilla extract

160 g (5¾ oz) plain flour

½ teaspoon bicarbonate of soda

generous pinch of salt

100 g (3½ oz) milk or dark chocolate, roughly chopped

vanilla ice cream, to serve (optional)

METHOD

1. Preheat the oven to 180°C (350°F), Gas Mark 4.

2. In a large bowl, combine the butter and both sugars until you have a smooth, thick paste. Add the egg, egg yolk and vanilla and mix until smooth.

3. Sift in the flour, bicarbonate of soda and salt, and mix once more. You should have a thick, sticky dough.

4. Fold through the chopped chocolate and form the dough into a large ball.

5. Butter an ovenproof frying pan or skillet and add the cookie dough. Flatten the dough with your hands and press it out to fill the base of the pan.

6. Transfer to the oven and bake for 12 minutes until the cookie is golden but still soft and gooey in the centre, with melting chocolate pieces.

7. Present the cookie in the pan with 4 large scoops of ice cream in the centre. Spoon the cookie and melting ice cream into bowls to serve. Alternatively, dive straight in with spoons for the ultimate sharer!

STRAWBERRIES & CREAM FUDGE

PREP TIME: **10 MINUTES +
  CHILLING**
COOK TIME: **5 MINUTES**
DIFFICULTY: **EASY**
SERVES: **10**
VEGGIE

If you're blessed with a sweet tooth, whip up this NAWTY pink white-choc-and-strawberry fudge in 15 minutes.

INGREDIENTS

knob of butter, for the tin

400 g (14 oz) white chocolate

400 g (14 oz) can of condensed milk

3 tablespoons strawberry milkshake powder

1 teaspoon pink food colouring

200 g (7 oz) strawberries–and–cream chocolate truffles

METHOD

1. Butter a 22cm– (8½–inch–) long loaf tin and line the base and sides with nonstick baking paper.

2. Melt the white chocolate in a heatproof bowl set over a saucepan of *very* gently simmering water, making sure the bowl doesn't touch the water. This should take about 5 minutes. (White chocolate has a high percentage of milk fats, giving it a lower melting point than milk and dark chocolate, so melting it over a very gentle heat means it won't burn and seize up.)

3. Meanwhile, whisk together the condensed milk, strawberry milkshake powder and pink food colouring in a small bowl.

4. Once the white chocolate has fully melted, stir in the condensed milk mixture until fully combined. Stir half of the truffles through the fudge mix, then pour it into the prepared tin.

5. Roughly chop the remaining truffles and sprinkle them on. Place in the refrigerator for at least 4 hours, or until firm.

6. Once set, turn out and slice into slabs to serve.

TIP:
Swap strawberry milkshake powder for chocolate flavour and swap the truffles for chocolates.

PREP TIME: **20 MINUTES +
CHILLING**
COOK TIME: **NONE**
DIFFICULTY: **EASY**
SERVES: **8–10**
VEGGIE

PARTY BISCUIT CHEESECAKE

Bring this to the next shubz for all the sweet vibes. LET'S GO.

INGREDIENTS

150 g (5½ oz) melted unsalted butter, plus more for the tin

500 g (1 lb 2 oz) iced ring biscuits

680 g (1 lb 8 oz) full–fat cream cheese

300 ml (½ pint) double cream

100 g (3½ oz) icing sugar

1 teaspoon vanilla extract

METHOD

1. Butter a 20 cm (8 inch) springform cake tin.

2. Put half the biscuits into a medium–sized bowl. Use a rolling pin to crush them to a fine crumb. Pour in the melted butter, mix and transfer to the prepared tin. Use the back of a spoon to press the crumb mixture tightly into the base of the cake tin. Put in the refrigerator to chill while you make the filling.

3. Put the cream cheese, double cream, icing sugar and vanilla extract into a large mixing bowl and whip for 2–3 minutes until thick and silky. Be careful not to over–whip, or the mixture will turn cakey in texture.

4. Remove the cake tin from the refrigerator. Spoon the cream filling over the biscuit base, top with the remaining biscuits and return to the refrigerator for at least 1 hour, until set.

5. Unlatch the springform tin and remove. Place the cheesecake on a board or plate and slice to serve.

SKY-HIGH BANAYNAY SUNDAE

PREP TIME: **5 MINUTES +
  FREEZING**
COOK TIME: **NONE**
DIFFICULTY: **EASY**
SERVES: **2**
VEGGIE

GET HIGH on sugar with this banging banaynay sundae. Literal flavours, towered with biscuits, cream, caramel sauce and our very own honeycomb (little recipe inception ting).

INGREDIENTS

6 large bananas

2 tablespoons honeycomb (for Caught's DIY Honeycomb, see pages 48–9), crumbled

6 speculoos biscuits, such as Lotus, roughly crushed

aerosol can of squirty cream

100 ml (3½ fl oz) shop-bought salted caramel sauce

50 g (1¾ oz) milk chocolate, roughly chopped

METHOD

1. Peel and slice the bananas and spread them out across a plate or tray. Cover with clingfilm and freeze for at least 3 hours. (Now would be a good time to make our DIY Honeycomb, if you are going to make your own.)

2. Once out of the freezer, put the chopped bananas into a food processor or high-powered blender and pulse to break up the slices. Scrape down the sides of the blender and continue to pulse until the banana thickens to a smooth, sticky, creamy paste.

3. Spoon the banana paste into an airtight container and freeze for another hour, or serve straight away if you like it on the softer side.

4. When ready to serve, scoop the banana ice cream into 2 tall glasses, crumbling the biscuits over the top as you go. Adorn with squirty cream, salted caramel sauce, a handful of chopped chocolate and the crumbled honeycomb. Dig in!

ICE-CREAM COOKIE SANDWICH

Since when did sandwiches get capped at salad and bread? RELAX. This cookie ice-cream sando will have the SWEET ONES drooling. No ragrets. For the sweeeet ice-cream filling, our faves are cookie dough, vanilla or chocolate.

INGREDIENTS

120 g (4¼ oz) unsalted butter, at room temperature

50 g (1¾ oz) light brown sugar

50g (1¾ oz) caster sugar

1 egg, plus 1 egg yolk, lightly beaten

1 teaspoon vanilla extract

160 g (5¾ oz) plain flour

½ teaspoon bicarbonate of soda

generous pinch of salt

100 g (3½ oz) chocolate chips

475 ml (17 fl oz) paper tub of ice cream

rainbow sprinkles, to serve

METHOD

1. Preheat the oven to 180°C (350°F), Gas Mark 4. Line a baking tray with nonstick baking paper.

2. In a large bowl, combine the butter and both sugars until you have a smooth, thick paste. Add the eggs and vanilla and mix until smooth.

3. Sift in the flour, bicarbonate of soda and salt, and mix once more. You should have a thick, sticky dough.

4. Fold through the chocolate chips and divide the cookie dough into 8 balls.

5. Lay the balls across the prepared baking tray and bake for 12 minutes, or until the cookies have spread out and are cooked with a soft centre.

6. Turn the tub of ice cream on its side and use a large, sharp knife to slice the ice cream into 4 rounds, tub and all, each about 2.5–5 cm (1–2 inches) thick. Peel away the carton from each slice and sandwich the ice–cream slices between the cookies.

7. Roll the edges of the cookie sandwiches in rainbow sprinkles and enjoy!

BANANA BOMB MUFFINS

PREP TIME: **10 MINUTES +
FREEZING**

COOK TIME: **25 MINUTES**

DIFFICULTY: **EASY**

MAKES: **12**

VEGGIE

These muffins are DA BOMB. Take a bite and prepare for the oozing melted choco surprise.

INGREDIENTS

12 teaspoons chocolate
hazelnut spread, such as
Nutella

4 ripe bananas

80 ml (2¾ fl oz) vegetable oil

1 egg

80 g (2¾ oz) brown sugar

80 ml (2¾ fl oz) milk

220 g (8 oz) self-raising flour

1 teaspoon bicarbonate of soda

METHOD

1. Spoon each teaspoon measure of the hazelnut spread separately across a plate, so each forms a 'truffle'. Place in the freezer to chill for half an hour until solid.

2. Preheat the oven to 190°C (375°F), Gas Mark 5 and line a muffin tray with 12 muffin cases.

3. Peel 3 of the bananas and mash in a large mixing bowl, then add the oil, egg, sugar and milk and mix until you have a smooth, runny batter.

4. Sift in the flour and bicarbonate of soda and fold through until well combined.

5. Divide the mixture between the prepared muffin cases. Push a solid hazelnut-spread truffle into each, ensuring the truffles are fully submerged.

6. Top each muffin with a slice of the remaining banana and bake for 20-25 minutes until risen and golden with an oozing centre. Enjoy while still warm.

CAUGHT'S CARROT CUPCAKES

PREP TIME: **10 MINUTES +** **CHILLING**
COOK TIME: **25 MINUTES**
DIFFICULTY: **EASY**
MAKES: **12**
VEGAN

The best way to eat carrots is in cupcake form. Fact.

INGREDIENTS

For the icing

250 g (9 oz) vegan non-dairy spread/margarine

400 g (14 oz) icing sugar

2 tablespoons plant-based milk

1 teaspoon vanilla extract

1 tablespoon freshly squeezed orange juice

For the cupcakes

2 large carrots (about 300 g/10½ oz), peeled

juice of ¼ lemon

125 ml (4 fl oz) vegetable oil

80 ml (2¾ fl oz) plant-based milk

200 g (7 oz) light brown sugar

220 g (8 oz) plain flour

1 teaspoon baking powder

1 teaspoon ground cinnamon

50 g (1¾ oz) chopped walnuts, plus more to decorate (optional)

METHOD

1. To make the icing, put the vegan spread, icing sugar, milk, vanilla extract and freshly squeezed orange juice into a large bowl and whisk for 1–2 minutes until light, fluffy and holding its shape. Cover and set aside in the refrigerator to chill.

2. Preheat the oven to 180°C (350°F), Gas Mark 4 and line a muffin tray with 12 cupcake cases.

3. Finely grate 30 g (1 oz) of the carrots. Squeeze the lemon juice over the top to stop the grated carrot from discolouring, then cover and set aside in the refrigerator. (This will be used to garnish the cupcakes.)

4. Grate the remaining carrot, using the coarse side of the grater for chunkier pieces. Put into a large mixing bowl and combine with the vegetable oil, plant milk and light brown sugar.

5. Sift in the plain flour, baking powder and cinnamon and stir through until well combined. Fold through the chopped walnuts, if using.

6. Spoon the cake batter into the prepared cupcake cases. Bake for 25 minutes until risen and golden.

7. Remove from the oven and transfer the cupcakes to a wire rack to cool. When cool, smooth a spoonful of icing over the top of each cupcake and garnish with the reserved carrot and chopped walnuts, if using. Serve immediately, or store in an airtight container in the refrigerator for up to 3 days.

JAFFA CAKE BREAD & BUTTER PUDDING

Bread-and-butter pudding ELEVATED with a little jaffa cake goodness; you'll have the gang queuing down your road for a piece of this pud.

INGREDIENTS

25 g (1 oz) salted butter, at room temperature

1 small brioche loaf, thickly sliced

20 jaffa cakes

500 ml (18 fl oz) custard

2 eggs, lightly beaten

80 ml (2¾ fl oz) milk

1 tablespoon icing sugar, to dust (optional)

METHOD

1. Preheat the oven to 180°C (350°F), Gas Mark 4.

2. Butter the slices of brioche and halve them diagonally. Stand the triangular slices upright in a 20cm (8–inch) square baking tin and slot the jaffa cakes in between. Reserve 2-3 jaffa cakes to crumble over the top.

3. In a medium bowl, combine 400 ml (14 fl oz) of the custard with the eggs and milk, whisking to a smooth batter. Pour this over the brioche slices and jaffa cakes.

4. Chop up the reserved jaffa cakes and sprinkle over the top.

5. Cover with foil and bake for 10 minutes, then remove the foil and return to the oven for a further 2-5 minutes. The brioche should be lightly crisp and golden and the chocolate on the jaffa cakes melting.

6. Dust over the icing sugar, if you like, and serve with the remaining custard poured over.

TIRAMISU BROWNIE BITES

PREP TIME: **30 MINUTES +
COOLING + CHILLING**

COOK TIME: **25 MINUTES**

DIFFICULTY: **EASY**

MAKES: **16**

VEGGIE

As if brownies could be ANY MORE sensational... they can! Especially when a little juice is involved, you get me? Tiramisu means 'pick me up' and trust, these bites will bring good vibes.

INGREDIENTS

For the brownies

70 g (2½ oz) salted butter, cubed

100 g (3½ oz) dark chocolate, roughly chopped

100 g (3½ oz) caster sugar

100 ml (3½ fl oz) coffee liqueur, suitable for vegetarians

1 egg, plus 1 egg yolk, lightly beaten

40 g (1½ oz) plain flour

For the rest

300 ml (½ pint) double cream

125 g (4½ oz) mascarpone

25 g (1 oz) icing sugar

90 g (3¼ oz) sponge fingers (about 18)

150 ml (¼ pint) strong espresso coffee, cooled to room temperature

cocoa powder, to dust

METHOD

1. Preheat the oven to 180°C (350°F), Gas Mark 4. Line a 20cm (8-inch) square brownie tin with nonstick baking paper.

2. Melt the butter and chocolate together in a heatproof bowl set over a saucepan of gently simmering water, making sure the bowl does not touch the water. Once melted, remove the bowl from the heat and stir in the caster sugar and half the coffee liqueur.

3. Allow the mixture to cool a little, then stir in the eggs and flour, ensuring the mixture is smooth.

4. Transfer the mixture to the prepared tin and bake for 20-25 minutes, or until a skewer inserted into the middle comes out clean. Allow the brownie to cool in the tin.

5. Put the cream, mascarpone, remaining liqueur and icing sugar into a large bowl and whip for about 1 minute, or until thick and holding its shape.

6. Dip the sponge fingers in the espresso and lay across the top of the cooled brownies, still in the tin. Spoon over the boozy cream mixture and dust with cocoa powder.

7. Chill in the refrigerator, removing 30 minutes before serving. Slice into 16 small squares and enjoy!

PREP TIME: **10 MINUTES +
FREEZING**

COOK TIME: **NONE**

DIFFICULTY: **EASY**

SERVES: **4**

VEGGIE

NO-CHURN ICE CREAM

Who has time to be churning ice cream? Once you make this, you'll want to quit the day job and get your own ice-cream van.

INGREDIENTS

70 g (2½ oz) chocolate
  milkshake powder

200 g (7 oz) condensed milk

600 ml (20 fl oz) double cream

To serve (optional)

shop-bought chocolate sauce

shop-bought salted caramel
  sauce

glacé cherries

METHOD

1. Put the chocolate milkshake powder, condensed milk and double cream into a large mixing bowl and whip for about 5 minutes using an electric whisk, until thick. Transfer the mixture to a 22cm– (8½–inch–) long loaf tin and store in the freezer for 6 hours, or until frozen.

2. Serve in scoops, drizzled with chocolate and salted caramel sauce, and topped with glacé cherries, if you like.

PREP TIME: **20 MINUTES +
FREEZING**
COOK TIME: **10 MINUTES**
DIFFICULTY: **EASY**
MAKES: **10-12**
VEGAN

WATERMELON ICE POPS

Whip up some summer VIBES with these fruity frozen watermelon pops! Store in the freezer for them tropical days. You'll need lolly moulds and wooden lolly sticks for these.

INGREDIENTS

75 g (2¾ oz) caster sugar
40 ml (1½ fl oz) water

1 baby watermelon (approx. 1 kg, 2 lb 4 oz)
4 kiwis (approx. 225 g, 8 oz)

METHOD

1. Put the sugar into a small saucepan. Pour over the measured water and give the pan a gentle shake to ensure that the sugar and water are spread evenly across the base. Place the saucepan over a low heat and allow the sugar to melt. *Do not stir* or the sugar may crystallise, leaving you with a cloudy syrup. After 5-10 minutes, the sugar should have dissolved into the water, giving a clear liquid. Set aside.

2. Halve the watermelon and spoon out the flesh into a food processor. Pour in the sugar syrup and blend until smooth.

3. Pour the watermelon purée into ice-lolly moulds, leaving a gap of about 2cm (¾ inch) at the top for the kiwi purée. Push in the lolly sticks and put in the freezer to chill for 2 hours.

4. Meanwhile, rinse out the food processor, then halve the kiwis, spoon in the flesh and blend to a smooth, thick purée. Set aside in the refrigerator until the ice lollies have started to set.

5. Spoon the kiwi purée into the ice-lolly moulds over the watermelon and return to the freezer for a further 6 hours, or overnight. Serve and chill.

TIP:
Don't have ice-lolly moulds? Use small glasses instead.

CAUGHT SIPPIN'

CAUGHT DRINKIN' GAMES

Turn up (responsibly) at the shubz with Caught's favourite drinking games.

FIVES

Get the group sitting in a circle, each with one hand in a fist in the middle like spiritual tings.

Take it in turns to say a multiple of five (up to the number of people present, so if you have three players the max is 15, for four players the max is 20, and so on). The person guessing says their number on the count of three, at the same time that everyone either opens up their hands or keeps them clenched.

Open hands = 5, closed fists = 0.

If you guess the correct number, you're out of the game, but if you're incorrect, you must drink, and carry on playing.

If you're the last person in the game, you have to drink five fingers of your drink. It's a bit nuts, I can't lie.

TOP TIP: PRACTISE YOUR TIMES TABLES, YOU GET ME!

THE KILLER GAME

Bring your inner assassin to the shubz with this brutal (but 100 per cent safe) murder game.

Fill three hats with the names of people who are playing, objects and locations in the house. Pick one of each. Now 'kill' the person whose name you chose by handing them the object you picked in the location you chose without them realising. Think Cluedo tings, but more interactive.

WARNING: THIS GAME MAY GO ON FOR THE LONGEST.

BACK TO BACK

Time to dig all the madness you wouldn't dare to share sober.

Get two of your mates standing back to back and ask them questions. Go easy with 'Who is older?' or go in for a roast with 'Who has the deadest dress sense?'

Whoever thinks they are the answer needs to drink, not speak; if neither of them, or both of them, drink, they both have to drink again.

TOP TIP: THIS IS FUN WITH BEST MATES, COUPLES, ALMOST-COUPLES, EX-COUPLES, OR ANYONE WITH SOME UNRESOLVED BEEF.

BITES 'N' BEER PONG

Beer Pong meets *Man v. Food*.

Put a fun twist on a firm favourite by adding bowls of food into your beer-cup formation on a table. Throw a ping-pong ball – from the other end of the table – aiming at the bowls and cups. Then drink (or eat) what you landed in.

Make it nasty (with inspo from our ILLEGAL food combos on Caught Snackin's YouTube) or keep it nice – up to you...

WARNING: THE WORSE THE FOOD COMBOS, THE MORE MATES YOU'LL LOSE.

THE HAT GAME

Fan of charades? Get ready for the level up.

Get into teams and fill a hat with names (think celebs, or spice it up by choosing people in the group). Take it in turns to pick out names and act out or describe the person (without saying their name). Get your team to guess as many as they can in a minute.

Not as much of a mazza as the killer game (*above left*), but definitely sure to stress a few man out.

WARNING: MAY CAUSE BEEF AT THE SHUBZ.

FLIP CUP

Yeah, people train for the Olympics... But no sport is as extreme as Flip Cup. THIS IS SERIOUS.

Split the group into two teams (keep those athletic ones on your side). Fill your cups in two rows along either side of the table and stand behind them.

The first member of each team must down their drink, and put their empty cup upside down over the edge of the table. They then need to use the back of their hand to flip the cup so it's the right way up on the table, before the next person can down their drink and repeat. The team to finish first wins.

WARNING: I BEG YOU LOT, DON'T PLAY THIS WITH GLASS CUPS.

DON'T SAY IT

This one's easy, but effective.

Write up a list of words which are banned for the evening (use our glossary, on pages 8–9, if you want). Every time someone says one of those words, they have to drink.

TOP TIP: INCLUDE WORDS LIKE 'DRINK', 'GLASS', 'FOOD', 'MEAL' FOR MAXIMUM RESULTS, AND YOU'LL BE DRUNK BEFORE THE MAIN COURSE. (BUT PLZ BE CAREFUL.)

DISHWASHER GUMMY-BEAR VODKA

PREP TIME: **10 MINUTES + DISHWASHER CYCLE + CHILLING**

COOK TIME: **NONE**

DIFFICULTY: **EASY**

MAKES: **25 SHOTS**

VEGGIE

If you guys follow us on TikTok, you'll know about this MAD cheeky bev! However, the gummy bears be making a cameo appearance! Sweet and strong. Just like me.

INGREDIENTS

70 cl (1¼ pint) bottle of vodka, suitable for vegetarians

400 g (14 oz) veggie gummy bears, or your favourite gummy sweets

METHOD

1. Measure 300 ml (½ pint) of the vodka into a spare jar or bottle and keep for another occasion. This will allow space for the gummy bears.

2. Push the gummy bears into the vodka bottle and secure the lid.

3. Place the bottle in an empty dishwasher and run it on a 'quick' or 'eco' cycle, without using dishwasher detergent.

4. The dishwasher cycle will heat the vodka without cooking off the alcohol (important!) and allow the gummy bears to infuse and flavour the drink.

5. Chill before serving. There will be a bit of vodka-infused-melted-gummy-bear-sugar-goo at the bottom of the bottle, so strain that out, if you like. Or not.

LEMON JELLY SHOTS

PREP TIME: **10 MINUTES + CHILLING**
COOK TIME: **NONE**
DIFFICULTY: **EASY**
SERVES: **16 (makes 32 wedges)**
VEGGIE

Dangerously GOOD lemon jelly shots, slurped from lemon-skin cups to turn the level up at the shubz. Jelly isn't usually suitable for veggies, so you'll have to look for veggie-friendly jelly if you need these shots to be.

INGREDIENTS

8 lemons
135 g (5 oz) packet of vegetarian lemon–flavoured jelly
285 ml (9½ fl oz) boiling water
125 ml (4 fl oz) limoncello, suitable for vegetarians

METHOD

1. Halve the lemons lengthways and carefully scoop out the flesh so that you are left with the hollow skins. Juice the flesh and save the juice for another occasion.

2. Separate the jelly into cubes, putting these into a medium-sized bowl. Pour over the measured boiling water and stir until the jelly has dissolved. This should take about 5 minutes.

3. Stir in the limoncello and pour the mixture into the lemon–skin cups. Place in the refrigerator for at least 2½ hours to set.

4. Once set, slice each lemon cup in half to make lemon wedges.

TIP:
Throw some oranges and limes into the mix. Simply swap the jelly flavours accordingly or mix and match.

PREP TIME:
5 MINUTES EACH
COOK TIME: **NONE**
DIFFICULTY: **EASY**
SERVES: **1**
VEGGIE

SPICY-HOT BLOODY MARY

Word on the street is that if you say 'Bloody Mary' three times, a cocktail will appear! If it doesn't, then you shouldn't be so gullible; go make this recipe yourself.

INGREDIENTS

1 packet of spicy-hot corn puffs
juice of 1 lime
handful of ice
50 ml (1¾ fl oz) vodka, suitable for vegetarians
½ teaspoon hot sauce
½ teaspoon vegetarian Worcestershire sauce
¼ teaspoon pepper
175 ml (6 fl oz) tomato juice
1 celery stick

METHOD

1. Set aside a small handful of spicy-hot corn puffs to garnish and crush the rest to a crumb with a rolling pin. Put the spicy crumbs in a dish.

2. Squeeze half the lime juice on to a small plate and dip the rim of a tall glass in the juice, then dip it into the spicy-hot crumb.

3. Fill the glass with ice and add the vodka, hot sauce, Worcestershire sauce, pepper and tomato juice. Give it a stir with a stick of celery and enjoy!

Cocktails, cocktails, cocktails

RUM & COKE FLOAT

Get merry with this cheeky float. The sugary kick with the booze will make for some swashbuckling scenes, trust...

INGREDIENTS

large handful of crushed ice
50 ml (1¾ fl oz) dark rum, suitable for vegetarians
300 ml (½ pint) cola
2 scoops of vanilla ice cream
glacé cherry and lemon slice, to garnish (optional)

METHOD

1. Put the crushed ice into a tall glass and pour in the dark rum.

2. Top up with the cola and 2 scoops of vanilla ice cream.

3. Garnish with a cherry and a slice of lemon, if you like.

ENERGY MOJITO

Them ones where you're flagging at 5pm... This energy mojito will bring you right back to life, feeling the buzz.

INGREDIENTS

juice of 2 limes, plus a lime slice, to serve
½ teaspoon granulated sugar
3 mint sprigs
handful of crushed ice
50 ml (1¾ fl oz) white rum, suitable for vegetarians
250 ml (9 fl oz) energy drink

METHOD

1. Put the lime juice, sugar and mint leaves from 2 of the mint sprigs into a small bowl and crush with the end of a rolling pin until you have a loose, paste-like consistency.

2. Scoop a handful of crushed ice into a tall glass and pour over the mint mixture, followed by the white rum and the energy drink.

3. Give the mojito a good stir and garnish with the remaining mint sprig and the lime slice.

SPICY-HOT
BLOODY
MARY

ENERGY MOJITO

RUM & COKE
FLOAT

CINEMA SLUSHY

PREP TIME: **15 MINUTES +
  CHILLING**

COOK TIME: **NONE**

DIFFICULTY: **EASY**

SERVES: **2**

VEGGIE

**A RAINBOW slushy to complete
your movie night at home. Vibrant,
fruity and the perfect complement
to your popcorn, G – get on it!**

INGREDIENTS

350 g (12 oz) ice cubes

4 x 80 ml (2¾ fl oz) lemon–flavoured ice lollies

150 ml (¼ pint) red, cherry–flavoured fizzy pop

1 teaspoon pink food colouring

150 ml (¼ pint) blue–coloured fizzy pop

1 teaspoon blue food colouring

2 cherries, to garnish

METHOD

1. Wrap the ice cubes in a clean tea towel and bash with a rolling
   pin to crush into small pieces.

2. For the cherry–flavoured slushy, put 2 of the ice lollies (sticks
   removed) into a food processor with half the crushed ice, the
   cherry fizzy pop and the pink food colouring. Blitz the mixture
   repeatedly, in 5–second blasts, until you have a thick, slushy
   consistency. Transfer the mixture to a container and place in
   the freezer to chill while you make the blue slushy.

3. Repeat the process with the remaining ice lollies and ice, blue–
   coloured fizzy pop and blue food colouring.

4. Serve the slushies, layered up, in 2 tall glasses. Finish with a
   cherry and serve immediately.

MINT-CHOC FREAKSHAKE

PREP TIME: **15 MINUTES + CHILLING**

COOK TIME: **5 MINUTES**

DIFFICULTY: **EASY**

SERVES: **2**

VEGGIE

This shake gets pretty freaky. Mint on mint action with this SWEET ONE. Mint chocolate balls, mint ice cream, mint chocolate biscuits... Did we mention there's mint in here?

INGREDIENTS

100 g (3½ oz) dark chocolate, roughly chopped

2 x 92 g (3 ¼ oz) packets of peppermint–flavoured chocolate bubbles, such as Aero Bubbles

4 tablespoons rainbow sprinkles

5 scoops of mint–choc–chip ice cream

200 ml (7 fl oz) milk

aerosol can of squirty cream

2-4 mint chocolate–coated biscuits, such as Kit Kats or Clubs

METHOD

1. Melt the chocolate in a heatproof bowl set over a saucepan of gently simmering water, making sure the bowl does not touch the water. This should take about 5 minutes.

2. Crush 1 packet of peppermint–flavoured chocolate bubbles with a rolling pin, then place the pieces in a dish with the rainbow sprinkles.

3. Dip the rims of 2 tall glasses into the melted chocolate, then roll the rims in the dish to coat the chocolate with the bubbles and sprinkles. Carefully drizzle the remaining melted chocolate around the insides of the glasses. Place the glasses in the refrigerator to chill.

4. Put the remaining packet of mint–chocolate bubbles in a high–powered blender. Top with 3 scoops of the mint–choc–chip ice cream and the milk. Blend until smooth, then pour into the prepared glasses.

5. Top each glass with another scoop of mint–choc–chip ice cream, squirty cream, more crushed mint–chocolate bubbles and mint–chocolate biscuits, halved lengthways if you like. Serve immediately!

FROZEN
PASSION FRUIT MARTINI

These will BLESS your summer holiday by the pool. And if you're not on holiday, then this drink is the closest you'll get.

INGREDIENTS

2 tropical fruit–flavour ice–cream lollies, such as Solero
½ mango, peeled and cubed
50 ml (1¾ fl oz) vodka, suitable for vegetarians
100 ml (3½ fl oz) pineapple juice
1 passion fruit, halved

METHOD

1. Remove the sticks from the ice–cream lollies and put them into a high–powered blender, along with the mango, vodka and pineapple juice. Blend until smooth, then strain into 2 glasses.

2. Top each with a passion fruit half and enjoy.

FROZEN
ESPRESSO MARTINI

Ice-cold voddy coffee sprinkled with cocoa? Yes plz.

INGREDIENTS

100 ml (3½ fl oz) strong espresso coffee
large handful of crushed ice
50 ml (1¾ fl oz) vodka, suitable for vegetarians
100 ml (3½ fl oz) coffee liqueur, suitable for vegetarians
2 tablespoons caster sugar
cocoa powder, to dust (optional)

METHOD

1. Brew the espresso coffee and allow it to cool to room temperature.

2. Put the crushed ice, vodka, coffee liqueur, sugar and cooled coffee into a food processor or high–powered blender. Blitz in 5–second blasts until well combined.

3. Divide between 2 glasses and dust with cocoa powder, if you like.

Best sipped in the sunshine, but these taste great whatever the weather

PIÑA COLADA

PREP TIME: **5 MINUTES EACH**

COOK TIME: **NONE**

DIFFICULTY: **EASY**

SERVES: **2**

VEGGIE

If you like piña coladas... MAKE THIS. Pineapple and coconut rum blended with ice cream, topped with fruity garnish and of course a li'l umbrella for that beachside finesse.

INGREDIENTS

handful of crushed ice

150 g (5½ oz) frozen pineapple chunks

150 ml (¼ pint) coconut rum liqueur, suitable for vegetarians

75 g (2¾ oz) vanilla ice cream

To garnish (optional)

2 pineapple wedges

2 glacé cherries

pineapple leaves from a fresh pineapple

cocktail umbrellas

METHOD

1. Put the crushed ice, frozen pineapple, coconut rum liqueur and ice cream into a high-powered blender. Blitz in 5-second blasts until well combined with a smooth, thick consistency.

2. Divide between 2 large glasses and garnish each with a pineapple wedge, a glacé cherry, pineapple leaves and a snazzy umbrella, if you like.

FROZEN
PASSION FRUIT
MARTINI

FROZEN
ESPRESSO
MARTINI

FROZEN PIÑA COLADA

PREP TIME: **5 MINUTES**
COOK TIME: **2 MINUTES**
DIFFICULTY: **EASY**
SERVES: **2**
VEGGIE

HOT CHOCOLATE ORANGE MOCHA

When chocolate met orange, we were interested. When chocolate orange met coffee? Hold me back.

INGREDIENTS

300 ml (½ pint) whole milk

1 chocolate orange, such as Terry's

2 shots of espresso coffee

aerosol can of squirty cream

METHOD

1. Heat the milk in a small saucepan over a low heat for 2 minutes.

2. Break up the chocolate orange and finely chop 1 of the segments, setting this aside for garnish.

3. Remove the saucepan from the heat and add the rest of the chocolate orange segments. Stir the chocolate through the hot milk until completely melted and combined.

4. Pour the espresso coffee into 2 glasses and top with the hot chocolate orange mixture.

5. Finish with squirty cream and the finely chopped chocolate.

STRAWBERRY RICE PAPER BUBBLE TEA

PREP TIME: **5 MINUTES**

COOK TIME: **15 MINUTES**

DIFFICULTY: **EASY**

SERVES: **2**

VEGGIE

Bubble tea is WAY easier than you think with this secret magic. Just be sure to have a wide straw to slurp them LOVELY BUBBLES.

INGREDIENTS

400 g (14 oz) strawberries, stalks removed, halved

2 tablespoons caster sugar

2 tablespoons water

4 sheets of rice paper (sold as spring roll wrappers)

2 handfuls of crushed ice

500 ml (18 fl oz) milk

METHOD

1. Put the strawberries into a small saucepan with the caster sugar and measured water. Place over a low heat and bring to a gentle simmer. Simmer for 10 minutes, until the strawberries have broken down to a soft, mushy consistency. Remove from the heat and allow to cool.

2. Meanwhile, dip each of the rice paper sheets in lukewarm water so that they become pliable. Roll each sheet up tightly and slice into small 'boba' pieces, about 1 cm (½ inch) wide.

3. When the strawberry mixture has cooled, blitz in a food processor or high-powered blender until smooth. Pass the strawberry mixture through a sieve to remove any seeds.

4. Return the strained strawberry mixture to the small saucepan and add the rice paper boba. Simmer for 5 minutes. The boba will take on the pink colour of the strawberry mixture.

5. Divide the boba mixture between 2 tall glasses and top with crushed ice. Finish with milk and a wide straw to drink the bubble tea. Serve immediately!

TIP:

Biodegradable or reusable bubble tea straws are widely available online.

INDEX

UK-US Glossary

Aubergine – eggplant
Baking paper – parchment paper
Beef mince – ground beef
Bicarbonate of soda – baking soda
Biscuits – cookies
Caster sugar – superfine sugar
Chestnut mushrooms – cremini mushrooms
Chips – fries
Coriander – cilantro
Cornflour – corn starch
Crisps – potato chips
Double cream – heavy cream
Fish fingers – fish sticks
Fizzy pop – soda
Foil – aluminum foil
Granulated sugar – sugar
Green pepper – green bell pepper
Griddle pan – ridged grill pan
Grill – broiler/broil
Honeycomb – hokey pokey/cinder toffee/
    honeycomb candy/honeycomb toffee
Icing sugar – confectioners' sugar
Jelly – Jello
King prawns – jumbo shrimp
Kitchen paper – paper towels
Lamb mince – gounnd lamb
Pak choi – bok choy
Plain flour – all-purpose flour
Potato, Maris Piper – floury potato, such as a russet
Ready-salted crisps – classic potato chips
Red pepper – red bell pepper
Self-raising flour – self-rising flour
Spring onions – scallions
Stick blender – immersion blender
Stock – broth
Streaky bacon – side bacon
Sugar snap peas – snap peas
Yellow pepper – yellow bell pepper

ACKNOWLEDGEMENTS

BIG LOVE to our agents Lauren and Jo for believing in the Caught cookbook dream! When we first started playing around with recipes on TikTok, we never imagined they'd end up in a REAL-LIFE cookbook. MADNESS! Shoutout Lauren and Jo for making it happen for real!

But we couldn't have got here without the gang behind the scenes. Many blessings to Jason, Freya, Lydia, Harleigh and the whole Caught Snackin' team, who've worked so hard cooking and creating to bring this book to life.